A Leader's Guide

WE STILL HOLD THESE TRUTHS

*Rediscovering Our Principles,
Reclaiming Our Future*

JULY 4, 1776.
C. RESS. States of

The Heritage Foundation
214 Massachusetts Avenue, NE
Washington, DC 20002
(202) 546-4400
heritage.org

ISBN: 978-0-89195-136-0

TABLE OF CONTENTS

INTRODUCTION

B Y ANY MEASURE, THE UNITED STATES OF
AMERICA is a great nation. Thirteen colonies are now 50
states covering a vast continent and beyond. The United
States economy accounts for almost a quarter of the total gross
domestic product of all the countries in the world.

The strongest military force on Earth allows the U.S. to
extend its power anywhere. The American people remain among
the most hardworking, churchgoing, affluent, and generous. Just
as George Washington predicted, the United States is a sovereign
nation "in command of its own fortunes."

What accounts for this success?

Every nation derives meaning and purpose from some unifying quality – an ethnic character, a common religion, a shared
history. America is different. Unique among nations, America
was founded at a particular time, by a particular people, on the
basis of a particular idea.

At its birth, this nation justified its independence by asserting
truths said to be self-evident, according to "the Laws of Nature
and Nature's God." Working from the great principle of human
equality, the revolutionaries who launched this experiment in
popular government claimed a new basis of political legitimacy:
the consent of those governed. Through a carefully written constitution, they created an enduring framework of limited government based on the rule of law.

With this structure, they sought to establish true religious
liberty, provide for economic opportunity, secure national
independence, and maintain a flourishing society of republican
self-government – all in the name of a simple but radical idea of
human liberty.

In many circles today, especially among the learned of our
universities and law schools – those who teach the next generation, shape our popular culture, and set the terms of our political
discourse – the self-evident truths upon which America depends
have been replaced by the passionately held belief that no such

truths exist, certainly no truths applicable to all time. Over the past century, under the influence of progressivism and modern liberalism, the federal government has lost much of its grounding, and today acts with little regard for the limits placed upon it by the Constitution, which many now regard as obsolete.

This view now dominates the academy, the media, intellectual elites, and major portions of the leadership in both political parties. As a result, we are left divided about our own meaning as a nation, unable – perhaps unwilling – to defend our ideas, our institutions, and maybe even ourselves.

There is another way forward. But it will take a monumental effort to get our country back on track.

We don't need to remake America, or discover new and untested principles. The change we need is not the rejection of America's principles but a great renewal of the foundational principles and constitutional wisdom that are the true roots of our country's greatness.

In the midst of the many other challenges we face – unsustainable federal spending and increasing debt, the future burden of social welfare entitlements, national security in a dangerous world – the real crisis tearing at the American soul is not a lack of courage or solutions as much as a loss of conviction.

We must look to the principles of the American Founding – its philosophical grounding, practical wisdom, and limitless spirit of self-government and independence – not as a matter of historical curiosity but as a source of assurance and direction for our times.

Do we still hold these truths? Do the principles that inspired the American Founding retain their relevance in the 21st century? We will find it difficult to know what to do and how to do it as long as we are not sure who we are and what we believe.

We must restore America's principles – the truths to which we are dedicated – as the central idea of our nation's public philosophy. But before we can rededicate ourselves as a nation to these principles, we must rediscover them as a people. Only when we know these principles once again can we renew America.

–Dr. Matthew Spalding
  Director of the B. Kenneth Simon Center for American Studies,
  The Heritage Foundation

The things I want to know are in books. – Abraham Lincoln

IN THE UNITED STATES, THE PEOPLE are sovereign over their government. When a group of citizens study the principles and practices of their nation and its government, that is the first and most important step in the advancement of those principles and the restoration of constitutional government. This *Leader's Guide* is a companion to *We Still Hold These Truths*. It provides everything you need to take your group on a journey through history to discover what defines us as a nation, asking thought-provoking questions to get our country back on track.

HOW TO USE THE GUIDE

In these politically turbulent times, *We Still Hold These Truths* is an ideal book for reading and discussion groups. Here are some tips for a successful group study:

- The ideal size of a *We Still Hold These Truths* reading group should be between five and 10 members. Keeping your group to a reasonable number will allow for robust discussion and focused conversation.

- While only the group facilitator needs the *Leader's Guide*, everyone in the group needs a copy of *We Still Hold These Truths*. Be sure your group has read the necessary book passages indicated in the *Leader's Guide* before each meeting.

- The *Leader's Guide* is broken into 10 sessions, plus a conclusion chapter, so plan for an 11 week study. Each session should take 45-60 minutes to complete. If your group cannot meet for a full 11 weeks, plan to do the six Core sessions as they provide the fundamentals for your group.

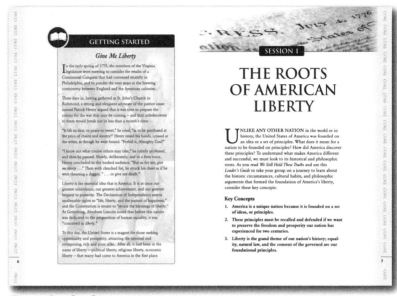

Example of a Core session.

- Short on time? Plan to do the Speed Round in each session. These passages are marked by this special icon in each session.

- Each session opens with a historical story from the book. You can choose to read these in advance to serve as background to lead your group. Or you can choose to duplicate and provide copies to your group. A downloadable copy of the *Leader's Guide* is available at WeStillHoldTheseTruths.org.

- Each session is broken down into individual sections that correspond to passages in the book. You can read the passages at the beginning of each section aloud to your group or review in advance and put in your own words. From there, jump right into the discussion questions with your group.

- At the end of each session, you'll find one single question identified as "Go Deeper." These questions challenge your group to apply the timeless principles presented in the book to the current debate today. Be sure to pace your group to allow more time to have a discussion about these questions.

If You Are Using the *Leader's Guide* for Self Study...

The *We Still Hold These Truths Leader's Guide* is a handy resource to solidify and clarify the book's teaching – augmenting a general education, refreshing an education now forgotten, or facilitating a fresh study of core concepts long overlooked but once again at the heart of public debate. Be sure to go at your own pace and spend extra time in the "Go Deeper" section where you can draw prompt connections between the ideas in the book and contemporary events.

If You Are a Parent or Student...

For the student, the book and *Leader's Guide* can be used as a supplemental text and study companion for a class on American government, American political thought or American history. It can also be used as a surrogate for material not covered and classes not offered. In this case, the book and study guide will aid the student in their course of study, regardless of their school, professors, or other barriers to their education. You can follow the same format as those using it in a small group setting or customize it to your own needs.

For more resources visit WeStillHoldTheseTruths.org.

Give Me Liberty

In the early spring of 1775, the members of the Virginia legislature were meeting to consider the results of a Continental Congress that had convened recently in Philadelphia, and to ponder the next steps in the brewing controversy between England and the American colonies.

Three days in, having gathered at St. John's Church in Richmond, a strong and eloquent advocate of the patriot cause named Patrick Henry argued that it was time to prepare the colony for the war that may be coming – and that unbeknownst to them would break out in less than a month's time.

"Is life so dear, or peace so sweet," he cried, "as to be purchased at the price of chains and slavery?" Henry raised his hands, crossed at the wrists, as though he were bound. "Forbid it, Almighty God!"

"I know not what course others may take," he calmly professed, and then he paused. Slowly, deliberately, and in a firm voice, Henry concluded to the hushed audience, "But as for me, *give me liberty . . .*" Then with clenched fist, he struck his chest as if he were thrusting a dagger, " . . . or give me death."

Liberty is the essential idea that is America. It is at once our greatest inheritance, our greatest achievement, and our greatest bequest to posterity. The Declaration of Independence asserts unalienable rights to "life, liberty, and the pursuit of happiness," and the Constitution is meant to "secure the blessings of liberty." At Gettysburg, Abraham Lincoln noted that before this nation was dedicated to the proposition of human equality, it was "conceived in *liberty*."

To this day, the United States is a magnet for those seeking opportunity and prosperity, attracting the talented and enterprising, rich and poor alike. After all, it had been in the name of liberty – political liberty, religious liberty, economic liberty – that many had come to America in the first place.

THE ROOTS OF AMERICAN LIBERTY

U NLIKE ANY OTHER NATION in the world or in history, the United States of America was founded on an idea or a set of principles. What does it mean for a nation to be founded on principles? How did America discover these principles? To understand what makes America different and successful, we must look to its historical and philosophic roots. As you read *We Still Hold These Truths* and use this *Leader's Guide* to take your group on a journey to learn about the historic circumstances, cultural habits, and philosophic arguments that formed the foundation of America's liberty, consider these key concepts:

Key Concepts

1. America is a unique nation because it is founded on a set of ideas, or principles.

2. These principles must be recalled and defended if we want to preserve the freedom and prosperity our nation has experienced for two centuries.

3. Liberty is the grand theme of our nation's history; equality, natural law, and the consent of the governed are our foundational principles.

4. Religious liberty and economic opportunity flow from these foundational principles; the rule of law and constitutionalism define the architecture that undergirds our liberty.

5. All of these principles that contribute to self-government and independence encompasses the meaning of America's principles in the world.

6. The roots of American liberty are the means by which the American Revolution resulted in peaceful self-government, in contrast to the violent overthrow and dictatorship of the French Revolution.

7. These roots are found in America's British heritage, religious faith, intellectual ideas, and experience in self-government.

8. America is the product of the moderate Enlightenment philosophers such as John Locke, Montesquieu, and William Blackstone, rather than the French radical Enlightenment philosophies that led to the French Revolution.

1 Introduction (pp. 1-6)

AMERICAN EXCEPTIONALISM
The idea that America is unique and has had exceptional success as a nation because it remains dedicated to certain universal principles.

For generations, people of all nationalities have recognized the uniqueness of America — often called "American exceptionalism." America is not exceptional or unique because of its location or ethnicity, but because of its foundation in a set of shared ideas and principles. Yet, over the last few generations we have forgotten those shared principles on which our nation was founded. As a result, we have lost our meaning and purpose. As Matthew Spalding writes, "this is not simply a case of national amnesia." The distressing state of our current politics "signals a larger systemic problem." To reclaim our politics, we need to recall these first principles and understand why we have strayed from them.

QUESTIONS

1. **What does the difference between the Roman Pantheon and the U.S. National Archives represent?**

   The Pantheon is dedicated to honoring military rulers and political power, while the National Archives honors the documents that set forth the principles and ideas guiding our nation. One recognizes force; the other, ideas.

2. **What is the book saying about the decline of our knowledge of history? How is this related to confusion about our core principles?**

   The problem is not just that we no longer learn history, but that we have replaced our belief in self-evident truths with relativism and a lack of confidence in our principles.

3. **Every nation thinks of itself as "exceptional" in some way or another, but what is unique about America's understanding as it relates to citizenship?**

   Contrary to all other nations, American citizenship is founded on shared principles, rather than race, ethnicity, or religion.

> **RELATIVISM**
> The idea that there is no permanent or certain truth but only relative truths that are always variable and contingent upon particular circumstances, such as time, place, or personal values.

2 The Cause of Liberty (pp. 7-10)

Liberty is the central concept and idea of America. Liberty does not mean the freedom to do whatever we want. In fact, the Founders saw an important distinction between liberty and freedom. Freedom denotes a lack of restraint: for instance, animals are free but not at liberty. Liberty is the rightful exercise of freedom, within the limits of a moral order reflecting natural law. From the Founders' viewpoint, liberty must be understood within the context of constitutional and moral order.

> "Liberty is the rightful exercise of freedom, within the limits of moral order reflecting natural law."

QUESTION

1. **What is the distinction between liberty and freedom? How does the distinction between the two illustrate the American understanding of liberty?**

Freedom is all-encompassing, and tends to emphasize a lack of restraint, but liberty implies responsible freedom — men and women acting according to human nature. The American view of liberty is bound by a moral order of right and wrong called natural law.

3 The Roots of American Liberty

(pp. 10-12)

America's British heritage is a crucial foundation of American liberty. More than anything else, the American colonies reflected their British roots, in their language, manners, customs, habits, and even form of government. These roots established cultural unity and common habits of government that made self-rule possible. They learned from the mistakes of British history and sought to improve upon the British constitution while not abandoning its tried and true forms of government.

QUESTION

1. **Why is it important that America had a common culture based on British roots?**

American liberty was an outgrowth of experience under the British Constitution, which was slowly embracing government by consent and the protection of individual liberties. Also, Americans' shared culture and language allowed them to deliberate in common about political goals.

4 God and Liberty (pp. 12-15)

Americans' shared religious faith was the most formative influence shaping the American concept of liberty. Many colonists came to America in search of religious liberty, and their faith was central to their self-government. Contrary to many scholars, almost all of the Founders were firmly in the mainstream of religious belief: God is the Creator of humanity, having endowed each person with an immortal soul, and maintains an active role in human affairs through his providence. This understanding of God led to very important consequences:

• God has created certain laws that exist prior to government, which government must observe.

• Man is created in the image of God. Man has an inborn dignity and a natural equality with other men.

• All men are sinners drawn to passion and selfish behavior; no person ought to hold absolute power.

• All men are redeemable. They are capable of governing themselves and acting with justice and charity toward one another.

QUESTIONS

1. What was the kind of faith that united both American colonists and the Founders?

The mainstream belief that God is the creator of human beings, the author of natural law, and is actively involved in human affairs.

2. How did this common faith influence the Americans' political ideas?

First, it established that there are natural laws that exist prior to human government; second, humans are created by God and thus have inborn dignity; third, humans are imperfect and ought not be trusted with absolute rule; fourth, redemption enables humans to be capable of self-government and virtuous action.

5 The American Mind (pp. 15-20)

Americans' views of liberty and justice were also shaped by their intellectual influences. The average citizen of the founding generation was literate and very well-read. The intellectual influences were wide – including the Bible, William Shakespeare, and John Milton, as well their own countrymen such as Thomas Paine and Thomas Jefferson. There were also classical influences, but very practical thinkers, such as Aristotle, Cicero, and Polybius. History, experience, and study – rather than abstract theory – taught them the principles of government. From the British sources, they learned the ideas of liberty; from classical (particularly Roman) sources they learned about natural law.

QUESTIONS

1. **How extensive were the intellectual influences on the founding generation?**

The influences were both classical and modern: from Cicero and Polybius to Shakespeare, Locke, and Milton. The founding generation also read history, which gave them experience to draw upon.

2. **How did the British tradition of liberty inform the Founders' intellectual influences?**

Beginning with Magna Carta, and through more recent documents such as the Petition of Right, Habeas Corpus Act, and English Bill of Rights, citizens of the founding generation learned that there were certain rights that ought to be protected by government.

6

The French Revolution; The American Enlightenment (pp. 20-24)

Americans were products of the Enlightenment. This meant that Americans possessed confidence that reason could answer important political questions to establish a more just and humane political order.

The French Revolutionaries were also products of the Enlightenment, but their revolution ended in massacre and a totalitarian regime. The French Revolution resulted from the extreme Enlightenment of the French *philosophes* – Diderot, Voltaire, and Rousseau – who rejected the concept of a fixed human nature and believed government could improve men.

By contrast, the American Founders were products of a moderate and practical Enlightenment, which believed in human nature as a permanent standard for politics. During the founding era, people read the Bible and writings by Enlightenment philosophers John Locke, Montesquieu, and Blackstone. The Founders followed England's republican tradition. Locke said government's role should be limited under the constitutional rule of law to the protection of the natural rights of all citizens. The differences between the two Enlightenments are still evident in the conservative/liberal distinction today.

ABSTRACT RATIONALISM
Unlike the more moderate enlightenment that supported scientific advance and maintained confidence that this reasoning would influence much of human life, abstract rationalism was an extreme version of enlightenment thinking that sought to overthrow every vestige of the existing political or social order and reconstruct society in accordance with abstract notions, such as the call for *liberté, égalité,* and *fraternité* during the French Revolution.

QUESTIONS

1. **What are the two versions of Enlightenment and what are their main differences?**

The moderate Enlightenment, which influenced the Founders, is based on practical reasoning and a fixed human nature as a guide for politics. The radical Enlightenment, which influenced the French Revolution, is based on abstract reasoning, a rejection of all tradition as prejudice, and the attempt to make a new man.

2. Who were the main figures of the two Enlightenments?

The main figures of the moderate Enlightenment were Locke, Montesquieu, and Blackstone. The main figures of the radical Enlightenment were Diderot, Voltaire, and Rousseau.

7 Colonial Experience (pp. 24-27)

The practical experience of governing themselves for 150 years without interference from the British Parliament deeply influenced the American understanding of liberty. Because the British generally neglected them, the American colonists learned to be self-sufficient and self-governing. Although the colonial charters provided governors and the king appointed executive officers, in most colonies the people elected at least one of the branches of the legislature. Thus the concept of representation developed in America, with each legislator representing his constituents but also seeking the common good. The experience in the colonies of self-rule taught Americans the importance of participatory government and being active in governing their own affairs.

QUESTIONS

1. How did practical experience inform the founding principles of America?

Because they were largely neglected by the British, the American colonists learned the importance of participation in civic life, managing their own affairs, and they picked up the habits of self-government.

2. How were the colonies' political institutions arranged, and how did that inform their ideas?

The King appointed many of the colonies' executive officers, but the colonists voted for representatives in their legislatures, which taught them the principle of representation through voting for officers.

3. How did American legislators differ from those in parliament?

In the British Parliament, the member stands for but does not represent constituents.

GO DEEPER

Today, America is increasingly diverse in its cultural and religious makeup. With their emphasis on common habits and culture derived from a long tradition of self-government, how would the Founders view our pluralistic society today? How best can we maintain the founding principles of this country in light of our pluralistic society? Are there any other ways in which Americans can be united, given our differences?

NOTES:

CORE CORE

SESSION 1

The Roots
of American
Liberty

CORE CORE CORE CORE CORE CORE CORE CORE CORE CORE CORE CORE CORE CORE

_____

_____

_____

_____

_____

_____

_____

_____

_____

_____

_____

_____

_____

_____

_____

_____

_____

_____

_____

_____

_____

From Loyalists to Revolutionaries

On the night of April 18, 1775, a force of British light infantry and grenadiers slipped out of their Boston encampment with the objective of seizing rebel military supplies thought to be hidden at Concord, Massachusetts. A well-organized team of riders, signaled by lanterns hung in the steeple of Boston's Old North Church and visible across the harbor, alerted the awaiting countryside. The British were coming.

On the way to Concord, in the predawn hours of April 19, the British force passed through the small village of Lexington. "Stand your ground," Captain John Parker told his volunteer militia. "Don't fire unless fired upon, but if they mean to have a war, let it begin here."

Upon entering Lexington that morning and seeing the armed colonials, the British forces quickened their march to a slow run. Major John Pitcairn of the Royal Marines charged up from behind and ordered the rebels to disburse. Moments later, shots were fired, then a series of volleys. The War for Independence had begun.

It was an amazing turnaround. Just a decade earlier, the British colonies in North America were a loyal part of the freest, richest, and most powerful empire that the world had ever known. Now they were in open revolt, and the king of England had declared them to be in rebellion. How had it come to this?

Between 1763 and 1776 the Americans were forced to think through fundamental questions about the basis of liberty and constitutional government. Key debates led to the definition of three closely connected foundational principles: that the just powers of government are derived from the consent of the governed; that the source of constitutional legitimacy is found in equal natural rights; and that these rights are grounded in the self-evident truth that all men are created equal.

WE HOLD THESE TRUTHS

I N SESSION ONE, we discussed the historical and philosophic roots of American liberty. Specifically, America's British heritage, religious faith, intellectual tradition, and experience in self-government, enabled America to create an independent, self-governing nation. The next few sessions (two through four) will focus on the foundational principles of liberty. Session two examines the bedrock principles of equality, natural rights, and consent of the governed articulated in the Declaration of Independence. To understand the profound importance of the Declaration, consider these key concepts:

NATURAL RIGHTS
Those fundamental rights possessed by every human person equally that are derived not from government but from our common human nature.

Key Concepts

1. The Declaration of Independence sets forth three closely connected foundational principles: consent of the governed, equal natural rights, and the self-evident truth that all men are created equal.

2. The Revolutionary War was not a mere tax revolt, even though the events were caused by the British tax policy. The most important issue for colonists was their objection to the British principle of "virtual representation," or government without consent.

3. During the debate over whether to declare independence from Great Britain, the colonists shifted from a justification in British tradition to grounding in natural law.

4. The sources for the colonists' turn to natural law were thinkers such as John Locke, William Blackstone, and Edward Coke, which meant that the American Revolution was not a break with the past, but drew upon ideas within their tradition.

5. The Declaration of Independence was addressed to the king because the colonists rejected the idea that Parliament had authority over them.

6. The truths expressed in the Declaration are self-evident, which means that they are always true, regardless of history or the circumstances of the time.

7. The existence of slavery was a contradiction to the founding principles; however, the Founders' prudent actions preserved liberty and put slavery on the course of extinction more effectively than a more radical approach would have.

8. The idea of nature, particularly a common human nature, forms the basis of the ideas of equality, human rights, and consent of the governed.

9. The Founders' idea of equality does not mean that everyone is equal in all respects, but that we all participate in a common human nature and rationality that separates us from other animals.

10. The idea of natural rights flows from the concept of human equality. Since we are all equal, we are all entitled to the basic rights that are derived from human nature.

11. The idea of the consent of the governed flows from the ideas of nature and equal rights.

1 The Road to Revolution (pp. 29-33)

In just a few years, the British colonies in North America went from loyal subjects to radical dissenters. How did this take place? There were essentially two causes – one theoretical and one practical. The practical cause was Great Britain's need to raise revenue after sustaining many expensive wars, the most immediate being the Seven Years' War which concluded in 1763. For the first time in many years, Britain looked to the colonies as a source of revenue to repay war debt. But this practical cause led to the true, theoretical cause: the British Parliament's assertion of power to bind the colonies "in all cases whatsoever," without their consent.

QUESTIONS

1. **What was the central issue that led to the Declaration of Independence?**

   The colonists' resistance to Britain was not only about taxation, but about British Parliament's assertion of exclusive legislative power in all cases over the colonies, despite colonial objections and lack of representation in Parliament.

2. **Why is it significant that the British repeal of the taxes on the colonies did not dispel the opposition to the crown?**

   The colonists were not upset over economic concerns as much as they insisted upon being able to govern themselves rather than being ruled by external authority.

2 Rights of Englishmen and of Nature

(pp. 33-36)

The colonists initially resisted the taxes imposed on them without their consent by appealing to their rights as Englishmen. But the dilemma was apparent. Since the King of England and the British Parliament defined the rights of Englishmen (because of the unwritten nature of the British constitution), this appeal left them at the

"The grounding of natural law provided the broadest and deepest support for the ideas that established America's political principles."

21

mercy of the very authority they were resisting. Therefore, almost from the beginning of the crisis, the colonists took the position that the British were wrong not as a matter of British law simply, but as a matter of natural law, which is unchangeable and built on the foundation of permanent nature. The grounding of natural law provided the broadest and deepest support for the ideas that established America's political principles.

QUESTIONS

1. What is the significance of the colonists' turn from appealing to the rights of Englishmen, to appealing to natural rights?

The appeal to natural rights provided a higher and permanent authority that could be used to judge government, rather than a system where the government decided right and wrong.

2. What were the sources of the idea of natural law as a foundation for political principles?

The sources were mostly British, primarily John Locke, and further shaped by their religious heritage.

> "What makes the Declaration revolutionary is not that it justified a rebellion, but that it established a new government on principles that were grounded in truth that is both permanent and transcendent, or God-given."

3 A Declaration of Independence

(pp. 36-39)

We celebrate July 4 as Independence Day because on that day the colonial leadership set forth the argument that justified the American Revolution. An appeal to principle, rather than force, justified our independence. The opening of the Declaration sets forth these principles:

- All men are created equal.

- They are endowed with natural rights that are inalienable, meaning those rights cannot be taken away or transferred.

- Government receives its just powers from the consent of the governed.

The body of the Declaration accuses King George III of many offenses against the colonies. The main charge against the king was his attempt to reduce the colonies to tyranny by establishing jurisdiction over them. What makes the Declaration revolutionary is not that it justified a rebellion, but that it established a new government on principles that were grounded in truth that is both permanent and transcendent, or God-given.

QUESTION

1. **What was the key charge against King George III found in the Declaration? How does this charge illustrate the crucial question of the American Revolution?**

   The key charge was that the king had conspired with Parliament to subject America to a "jurisdiction foreign to our constitution." Thus, the central issue of the American Revolution was whether the colonists would continue to govern themselves or be subject to the arbitrary rule of Britain.

4 The Laws of Nature and Nature's God (pp. 39-42)

The natural law concepts expressed in the beginning of the Declaration – equality, natural rights, and the consent of the governed – were not original. Jefferson admitted that he was merely stating what everyone in the colonies believed to be true: these ideas were "an expression of the American mind." But what did it mean to say that all men are created equal? It meant that all human beings are equal in their common human nature.

While there are many differences among human beings, there is still a common nature that distinguishes human beings from other animals. Other species follow instinct and are not rational; therefore, we do not hold them morally accountable. Humans have the ability to contemplate right and wrong and act accordingly. This distinguishes human beings from other animals and gives mankind the capacity for liberty. Furthermore, this understanding of human nature reaches back to classical philosophy and biblical theology and is consistent with the entire tradition of Western Civilization. The idea of human nature – this foundational concept to American liberty – is the result of a long tradition of Western thought.

QUESTIONS

1. **What is meant by the phrase that "all men are created equal"? How is this based on the idea of laws of nature?**

The idea that all men are created equal means that every person participates in a common human nature that distinguishes him from other animals and gives humans the capacity for reason and liberty. The laws of nature provide the design for human nature.

2. **What were the philosophical sources that influenced Jefferson when he wrote the Declaration?**

Jefferson and the Founders' concepts of human nature and natural law draw not only upon classical philosophy and biblical theology but also by moderate enlightenment thinkers such as John Locke and Algernon Sidney.

3. **What was the Founders' view of human nature?**

The Founders believed in a fallen human nature, which required devices to control rulers. Republican government, however, assumes that man has the ability to be virtuous. Thus, the Founders' sober view of human nature relied upon man to develop good character to correct human weakness.

5 Equal Rights (pp. 42-44)

The concept of nature formed the basis for all of the claims of the Declaration, including the idea of equal rights. In the Founders' view, because every human being participates in a common human nature, no human being is naturally so superior to other human beings that he can deprive them of their right to govern themselves. A right is something that justly belongs to someone and gives him a moral claim against anyone who would deprive him of that right. Moreover, an inalienable right is non-transferable; it cannot be voluntarily surrendered or involuntarily seized. This creates a corresponding duty for others to respect that right.

Because they are grounded in man's nature, natural rights are not open-ended; they do not lead to the radical multiplication of rights to mean anything and everything that someone might want. Moreover, government neither creates nor grants these rights. In fact, natural rights existed before government was created and act to restrain and check government. Government is not the source of rights and therefore may not legitimately deprive the people of their rights.

> "A right is something that justly belongs to someone and gives him a moral claim against anyone who would deprive him of that right."

QUESTIONS

1. **According to the Founders, what is a right and how does it flow from the idea of human nature and natural law?**

   A right is something that justly belongs to someone and creates a claim against anyone who would deprive him of that right. Rights are derived from the idea of a common human nature; since all human beings are equal in their essential nature, nobody may take away the natural rights of another.

2. **According to the Founders, what are man's natural rights and how has that understanding changed today?**

   According to the Founders, individuals only have rights to things that come from their nature – such as natural rights to life, liberty, property, and religious liberty. Today, our government operates by an unlimited view of rights, because personal will has replaced nature as the basis of rights.

6 The Contradiction of Slavery (pp. 44-47)

What are we to make of the existence of slavery in Colonial America? It is true that many, though not all, of the Founders owned slaves, and that they did not immediately end slavery. On the other hand, all of the Founders understood slavery to be naturally wrong, and believed that their principles would undermine slavery. Indeed, the central principle of the Declaration — natural human equality — was a rallying cry for the extinction of slavery. Moreover, we must consider how the Founders political achievements helped to end slavery. Many of the states immediately abolished slavery after the Constitution was passed, and by establishing one nation dedicated to human liberty and equality, the Founders laid the groundwork for the eventual ending of the institution of slavery.

> "The central principle of the Declaration – natural human equality – was a rallying cry for the extinction of slavery."

QUESTION

1. How did the Founders and their principles address the question of slavery?

Though some Founders held slaves, all of them understood slavery to be contrary to their principles and hoped to see it abolished over time as a result of their efforts.

7 The Consent of the Governed (pp. 47-50)

The principle of the consent of the governed follows from equality and natural rights. If we all equally participate in a common human nature, then no one naturally has a right to rule another; accordingly, government must be based on common agreement or consent. This was first termed "social compact," by thinkers such as John Locke, and was expressed in the Massachusetts Constitution of 1780, among other documents. By implication, government must be *created* by agreement and *operate* by consent.

The consent of the governed requires a popular form of government, but it does not mandate pure democratic rule. Rather, it means that popular *consent* be the basis for political governance. The Founders consistently maintained that the will of the majority is legitimate only if it rules so as to protect the rights of everyone – meaning, it must be the product of settled public reasoning consistent with the first principles of liberty.

QUESTIONS

1. How does the idea of the consent of the governed flow from the ideas of natural rights and equality?

Because all human beings equally participate in a common human nature, there are no natural rulers who can rule others without their consent. Government finds its legitimacy in popular agreement.

2. What does the idea of consent mean in practice?

First, government gets its initial power through consent or agreement, known as a "social compact." Second, government receives its ongoing power through consent, such that its policy is consistent with public opinion. Third, while it is not necessary for pure democratic rule, consent requires rule be in agreement with the first principles of liberty as expressed by public opinion.

"The consent of the governed requires a popular form of government, but it does not mandate pure democratic rule."

SOCIAL COMPACT

Since all men have equal rights and no one naturally has a right to rule another without their consent, just government arises out of our agreement or social compact.

GO DEEPER

Many people today look to the government to establish equality and level the playing field. How did the Founders view "equality" and how is this evident in the Declaration? Are there any differences between the Founders' understanding of rights and today's view?

NOTES:
_____

_____

_____

_____

_____

_____

_____

_____

_____

_____

_____

_____

_____

The Union of Faith and Freedom

In the fall of 1774, as the First Continental Congress was convening in Philadelphia, British military forces occupied the city of Boston and British naval ships filled Boston Harbor. Hostilities looked increasingly imminent, and a general sense of impending war weighed heavy on the delegates.

At such a trying moment, one of the delegates suggested that the members of the Continental Congress pray for divine guidance and protection. There were discussions, and then some debate. The members were divided in their religious denominations, what with Episcopalians and Quakers, Anabaptists, Congregationalists, and Presbyterians. Everyone seemed to disagree.

Then Samuel Adams, one of the early firebrands of the revolution, rose and said he would hear a prayer from anyone of piety and good character, as long as he was a patriot. And so the next morning an Episcopal clergyman led the members of the Continental Congress, ending with "an extraordinary prayer, which filled the bosom of every man present."

Nowadays, we are often told that religion is divisive and ought to be kept away from politics for the sake of liberty. Religion somehow is opposed to liberty, and so liberty requires a diminution of religion in the public square.

Among the American Founders, though, there was a profound sense that faith and freedom were deeply intertwined. "The God who gave us life, gave us liberty at the same time," Thomas Jefferson once wrote. "The hand of force may destroy, but cannot disjoin them."

All had a natural right to worship God as they chose, according to the dictates of their consciences. At the same time, the Founders advanced religious liberty so as to encourage religious faith and its moral influence on American self-government.

Religious liberty, and the proper understanding of the relationship of religion and politics, is a key principle of liberty.

OF FAITH AND REASON

The Establishment of Religious Freedom

IN THE PREVIOUS SESSION, we discussed the core principles of the Declaration of Independence – equality, natural rights, and the consent of the governed. In this session we will delve into religious liberty as a particular implication of these principles of equal, natural rights. As you read about the American conception of religious liberty, think about the following key concepts:

Key Concepts

1. The American establishment of religious freedom is a new solution to an old problem of the conflict between religious and political authorities.

2. For flourishing self-government, religion and civic virtues must be tightly linked together.

3. When political power is based on the consent of the governed and natural law, religious liberty is a citizen's right grounded in nature.

4. The American Founders brought about a practical solution to the conflict between reason and revelation. That solution was based on moral truths that harmonize with religion but which are capable of being discovered by reason alone.

5.   The American Founders recognized a space in which reason and faith can agree and cooperate. This allows different religions to work together on the basis of their common morality.

1 Failed Efforts to Reconcile Politics and Religion (pp. 52-55)

Historically, the American solution is new. In the ancient world, cities had their own gods, who were the source of all authority and law. Because gods were particular to a city, the political defeat of a city implied the defeat of its gods. Religious liberty was non-existent. Someone who did not believe in the gods of the city was considered a bad citizen.

Unlike any other people of the ancient world, the Hebrews embraced monotheism; they believed their God to be the *only* God, not just the strongest among many gods. Therefore, Jewish people retained their faith, even as a conquered nation.

"How does one reconcile the duty of citizenship with one's duty to God?"

Christianity transforms things because it claims that there is one true God for all men everywhere, regardless of their political allegiance. God rightly rules over all men, regardless of their origins or national allegiance. This claim creates a conflict: how does one reconcile the duty of citizenship with one's duty to God? In practice, pagan rulers, with laws derived from pagan gods, could not depend upon Christians' obedience. Christians consequently suffered much persecution.

In the Middle Ages, the doctrine of "two swords" divided power between religious and political authority. The political authorities had charge of earthly goods of the community; the church determined the spiritual direction of it. This solution proved problematic. Political authorities frequently pressured religious authorities with bribes, the use of force, or authoritarian powers. In return, the church could excommunicate political leaders, thereby removing any ties of loyalty toward the leader on the part of Catholic subjects.

After the Reformation, the "divine right of kings" argument (notably attacked by Locke in his *First Treatise on Civil Government*) was used to counter Catholic claims of papal authority over political rulers. During this period, the ruler generally determined the people's religion; there was, therefore, little freedom of conscience. This solution restrained international religious wars, but encouraged religious migration. Linking the religious faith of a people to their political authority increased the justification for religious persecution. Such persecution was widespread in 16th century England, leading its victims to seek a new land where they could worship God according to the dictates of their consciences. Thus, it was a desire for religious liberty – not fame and riches – that motivated many of America's first settlers.

> "It was a desire for religious liberty – not fame and riches – that motivated many of America's first settlers."

QUESTIONS

1. **How did the rise of Christianity challenge the pagan unity of political and religious power?**

   Christianity made a universal claim upon all humans to worship a God unconnected with any specific political society.

2. **What were the strategies used in the Middle Ages and the modern period to reduce the tension between the claims of political and religious authorities?**

   Initially, the "two swords" doctrine tried to divide power between political rulers and religious authorities. After the Protestant Reformation, the "divine right of kings" argument was used to justify religious independence of political rulers.

2 The Establishment of Religious Freedom (pp. 55-57)

Despite its many religious groups with deep theological differences, America was united by a common morality derived from a shared Judeo-Christian heritage and by the desire to escape religious warfare and religious persecution. Reason and the natural law – not doctrinal religious claims – provided the moral legitimacy for liberty and government in America. In this new political theory, all men are created equal, all men have natural rights, and government can only be legitimate if it is based upon consent. Among these fundamental rights of nature is the freedom of religion. Because the United States was based on the foundation of natural rights, it also protected the natural right to religious liberty.

The Founders distinguished between religious doctrines and political power. Government would protect the rights of conscience, without either coercing religious belief or promoting any particular religious doctrines. This did not mean a ban on public endorsement and encouragement of religion. In fact, President George Washington encouraged the exercise of religion. He wrote to the United Baptists that the rights of conscience would be protected, and Washington assured the Jewish congregation of Newport, Connecticut, that the "enlarged and liberal policy" of the United States required nothing from them but good citizenship in return for the protection of their natural rights. Political rights and the duties of citizenship are separate from religious belief and practice. The United States would accommodate any religion whose followers acted as good citizens.

Question

1. **How does the "enlarged and liberal policy" described by George Washington work in practice? Are there any limits to it?**

Religious differences are tolerated in a state of peaceful coexistence. Religious sects are free to worship as they see fit, so long as they respect the rule of law and participate in the shared responsibilities of citizenship.

3 A Common Morality (pp. 58-60)

Providing for religious liberty did not settle the competing claims of reason and revelation as an authoritative guide for life. The American solution is a *practical* rather than a *theoretical* solution. It establishes a government based on human nature and moral reasoning, the principles of which are available to all human beings. Equality, natural rights, and the consent of the governed do not require a special revelation to be understood, but merely the use of reason and common sense.

The Declaration of Independence contains a theological component, though. There is a natural rights theology that teaches rights are derived from "the Laws of Nature and of Nature's God." Other theological references in the Declaration are in biblical terms: God is the creator, the judge of the world, and acts in the world.

Thinkers throughout history have understood the natural law as a general revelation — as a revelation of God's law through nature and therefore accessible to reason. Washington, in his First Inaugural Address, declared that American policy must be based in private morality because of the link in nature between virtue and happiness.

The recognition of freedom of conscience by the American Founders (as with their argument for liberty itself) is not a grant of freedom from moral law. Moral law is derived from the permanent and unchanging natural law. The principles of natural law are in accordance with those of biblical religion, but can also be discovered by reason, independent of biblical revelation.

QUESTION

1. Is there a "theology" in the Declaration of Independence? What sort of claims does it make about the relation between man and God?

The Declaration of Independence speaks of "the Laws of Nature and of Nature's God" as the source of natural rights. Reason is sufficient to discover this. It also describes God as creator, judge, and providential guide. Man thus has a moral responsibility to his creator, whose providential hand guides the world.

4 Religion and Republican Government (pp. 60-64)

The Founders recognized that a self-governing nation must be a virtuous nation, and that religious faith is necessary. Different religions in America may compete on a theological level, but they cooperate on a political level by fostering a common morality. This is why Alexis de Tocqueville argued that religion is the first of America's political institutions. Religion shares similar concerns with government but does not formally operate in government. Thus, faith in the United States is free; no one religious doctrine is endorsed over another; and no religious test determines eligibility for political office. Separating religious authority from political authority does not weaken religion, but strengthens it. Separation from government means that religion is free from government control so it can form the conscience, shape society, and pursue its divine mission.

One cannot speak of religious liberty without discussing the First Amendment's Establishment Clause and Free Exercise Clause. The First Amendment forbids Congress from making any law regarding the establishment of religion. Congress can neither establish a national religion nor disestablish any of the state churches, such as those that existed in six of the 13 colonies. The Establishment Clause of the First Amendment was intended to *protect* religion from state control. The Free Exercise Clause guarantees the right to practice one's religion freely, provided that it does not violate any general laws.

Jefferson's famous phrase, "a wall of separation between Church & State," was not about removing religion from the public sphere. Jefferson uses the phase to explain why he thought it inappropriate to proclaim national days of fasting or thanksgiving. Not all Founders agreed with Jefferson. After Congress approved the Bill of Rights, Washington issued a proclamation calling for public thanksgiving to Almighty God for his many favors. Jefferson's comments did not prevent him from either attending religious services in Congressional chambers while president or allowing executive branch buildings to be used for religious purposes.

By all accounts, the First Amendment forbade certain actions on the part of the *federal* government, not the *state* governments. The Supreme Court, however, has misused this phrase and held that Jefferson's wall "must be high and impregnable," creating a far more radical separation than the Founders ever intended.

Religious faith has always been a crucial part of how we understand ourselves as a political community, from the references to God in the Declaration of Independence to the tax-exempt status of churches today. The Constitution allows for a general support of religion in public laws, speeches, ceremonies, and other public venues. These activities fall under the free exercise of religion, and have a practical benefit of promoting virtue.

"Jefferson's comments did not prevent him from either attending religious services in Congressional chambers while president or from allowing executive branch buildings to be used for religious purposes."

QUESTIONS

1. How did the Founders understand the relation between church and state?

The Founders recognized that a free people must be a virtuous people. Religion is the most effective method for developing the virtuous habits necessary for a people to live under a free government.

2. How did the Founders interpret the Establishment Clause of the First Amendment?

The Founders understood it as a limitation on the ability of Congress to establish a national church or disestablish the state churches that already existed in six of the 13 states. Moreover, it protected religion from being made an extension of the state.

5 The Flourishing of Faith and Liberty (pp. 64-65)

The Founders' protection of religious liberty was a practical solution to the historic conflict between the claims of reason and revelation. Political life was freed from sectarian tensions, and theology was freed from the temptation to involve itself in worldly matters. The American solution recognized that the claims of reason and of revelation can both be respected without either being secondary to political power.

> "The Founders' protection of religious liberty was a practical solution to the historic conflict between the claims of reason and revelation."

Second, natural law provides the basis for religious liberty and limited government. Government is limited to securing natural rights, above all the natural right to religious liberty.

Third, the Founders recognized that both political and religious authorities have an overlapping interest in morality. By separating theological questions from political questions, the Founders allow civic morality and religious morality to co-exist and even cooperate.

Lastly, religious liberty is an unalienable right because it concerns man's highest duty – his duty to his Creator. That pursuit develops a morally serious character, a necessary ingredient for free government.

QUESTION

1. How does the American institution of religious liberty strengthen both free government and religion?

The American solution is a practical rather than a theoretical solution. It allows government and religion to coexist without one or the other trying to gain the upper hand. Moreover, free government benefits from religious liberty insofar as religion is the most effective guarantor of a morally virtuous people.

GO DEEPER

Much is made these days of the so-called "separation of church and state." After studying the Founders' views on religious liberty, has your view of the current "wall of separation" changed?

NOTES: _____

_____

_____

_____

_____

Of Faith and
Reason: The
Establishment
of Religious
Freedom

Property, Properly Understood

In many ways, the right to property was the first principle at issue in the American Revolution. When the British began levying the first direct taxes on America, the colonists immediately considered it an unjust seizure of their property. "Can there be any liberty," wrote James Otis in a 1763 essay, "where property is taken without consent?"

Private property – not to mention the free-enterprise system for which it forms the foundation – is sometimes seen as the unfair prize of narrow self-interest, of undemocratic selfishness and greed that is incompatible with equality and the common good. The American Founders saw property (and so free enterprise) very differently. Property was understood not as a mere possession but as an integral component of freedom, deeply intertwined with and derivative of equal rights and human liberty itself.

Not only was it a requirement for securing the just rewards of labor – the key to a true free-market economy – and a necessary ingredient for economic prosperity, it was seen as a precondition for the enjoyment of other liberties and the cornerstone for building a commercial republic. If a man had a bit of property – a home, a piece of land, his own source of food and security – he could be independent, and so he could be free.

As the Founders saw it, the right to property was not simply an economic concept, and was much more than owning a bit of land. It was a first principle of liberty. In order to grasp the full breadth of the concept, think of property less as a static possession and more as the dynamic source of opportunity for all – the engine that allows liberty, prosperity, and civil society to flourish.

THE FIRE OF OPPORTUNITY

IN THE PREVIOUS SESSION, we discussed religious liberty as it arises out of the principles of equality and natural rights. As one of man's natural rights, freedom of religion demands government protection. We also discussed how religious liberty in turn provided political benefits, such as fostering the common public morality necessary to good citizenship. In this session, we will discuss the concept of private property as another implication of the principles of equality and natural rights. When thinking about the American Founders' protection of private property, consider the following key concepts:

Key Concepts

1. Property rights are indispensable to the individual rights to life, liberty, and particularly, the pursuit of happiness.

2. The right to obtain property is not the right to *have* any particular object of our desires — however important or needful those objects may be — but is the right to *pursue* such things.

3. The differences in the interests, abilities, and fortunes of human beings will inevitably lead to the unequal distribution of property.

4. The just enforcement of property rights through the rule of law results in a spirit of industry and enterprise on the part of the people because they are confident that they will be able to rightly enjoy the fruits of their labor.

FREE MARKET
A system of economic exchange in which individuals or groups voluntarily buy and sell goods at agreed upon prices. Unlike a controlled market, a free market is characterized by limited government intrusion beyond basic rule of law necessities.

"When property is withheld from the mass of society, the people become dependent on a privileged few."

PRIMOGENITURE
(prī-mō-'je-nə-chur)
The feudal rule that all inheritance is passed to the eldest son.

5. It is from the free operation of the marketplace, rather than the bureaucratic operation of a centralized government, that economic prosperity for the country as a whole is most likely to result.

6. Free market economies rely especially on the self-interest of individuals as the foundation of the prosperity of the nation.

7. The encouragement of individual self-interest through the protection of property rights and the free market economy lead to the civic virtues of industriousness and self-sufficiency required for a prosperous nation.

1 The Great Foundation of Property

(pp. 68-69)

There have always been distinctions among people in terms of property. That is to say, there have always been rich, poor, haves, and have-nots. For much of history, the few (i.e. kings, princes, lords) have held almost all property and wealth, resulting in widespread poverty and little or no prospect for advancement. Two common medieval practices reinforced the impoverishment of most people: primogeniture (inheritance falling to the eldest son) and entail (the inability to break-up and sell family property).

When property is withheld from the mass of society, the people become dependent on a privileged few. Because of this political problem, the American Founders, who were influenced by two advocates of private property – John Locke and Adam Smith – sought to place property rights with the individual. An important end of government is to secure the individual's natural right to obtain and make use of his property.

Questions

1. **What were the essential features and motivations of property laws prior to the American Founding?**

   Primogeniture and entail were aristocratic practices designed to concentrate and maintain property in the hands of the few. These practices prevented everyone else from acquiring or disposing of property.

2. **What is the distinctively different approach with respect to property taken by the American Founders?**

   To promote economic advancement for as many people as possible, the American Founders sought to make the opportunity to acquire, possess, and dispose of property available to everyone.

ENTAIL
The feudal rule that a family estate could not be broken apart or sold piecemeal.

2 First Principle of Association (pp. 69-71)

For property rights to be secure, individuals must be free not only to acquire and possess property but also to sell and dispose their property as they see fit. This is ultimately a matter of justice. Moreover, property rights are essential to the exercise of other civil rights, such as freedoms to publish, conduct business, and practice one's religious faith. Thus, securing property rights is a necessary step in securing the many other rights held by the people.

Question

1. **What is the relationship between property rights and other rights possessed by individuals?**

   Property rights are important to securing other individual rights. For example, private church property is a prerequisite to the free exercise of religion. Privately owned printers and publishers are prerequisites for freedom of the press.

"Property rights are important to securing other individual rights."

3 The Commercial Republic (pp. 71-74)

Although the Declaration of Independence lists the King's numerous violations of the colonists' property rights, Jefferson's famous listing of inalienable rights – life, liberty, and the pursuit of happiness – seems to omit property. This omission is not an exclusion; rather, the Founders understood property rights to be essentially intertwined with life, liberty, and the practical aspects of the pursuit of happiness. We seek to acquire those things (i.e. property) we think will fulfill our happiness. To be sure, we have a right to *pursue* these objects, not simply to *have* them. We might want a better home, but that does not mean that we have a right to have one.

Rights correspond to duties. Thus, our right to pursue a better home does not imply that the government, or some other group, has a corresponding duty to provide us with such a home. We do have the right to accomplish those things likely to result in our possession of a better home – control our own labor, enjoy the rewards of our work, save our money, etc. People have different opinions and abilities regarding the acquisition of property. There is diversity of opinion, because different people want different things – they have different interests. There is diversity of ability, because people have different levels of ambition and talents.

"The Founders understood property rights to be essentially intertwined with life, liberty, and the practical aspects of the pursuit of happiness."

QUESTIONS

1. **With respect to property, to what do individuals have a "right"?**

Individuals have a right to pursue property through the use of their own talent and industry. Individuals will sometimes succeed and will sometimes fail in their pursuit of property. One may contrast this with the view that individuals have a right to possess property, as if the possession of particular kinds of property were somehow guaranteed to the individual apart from individual effort or achievement; it is not.

2. The property rights in republican government result in the unequal distribution of property – how does this arrangement actually help the poor?

In an aristocracy, property is in the stagnant possession of a few. By contrast a republican government affords the poor the opportunity to use their industry to bring about a better future for themselves, their families, and their descendants.

The Foundation of Prosperity (pp. 74-76)

A society that champions property rights creates a spirit of enterprise, industry, and the incentive to work hard. This is because the people of such a society know that they will be able to keep what they earn, their property will not be confiscated through unjust laws, and the possibility for a better future for themselves and their children exists. When all of the economic players in a society (i.e. individuals, companies, large corporations) enjoy the protection of their property, the entire society's overall prosperity increases. Additionally, when government protects private property rights, individuals are more likely to follow their natural inclination to pursue their interests and happiness through their own labor. Therefore, everyone benefits from the protection of private property rights.

"A society that champions property rights creates a spirit of enterprise, industry, and the incentive to work hard."

QUESTION

1. How does protection of property rights lead to increased commercial activity and prosperity throughout society?

Protection of property rights invigorates individuals' industriousness and productiveness, because individuals trust that they will be able to keep their earnings and provide for a better future for themselves. This activity expands opportunity and prosperity for everyone.

CORE CORE CORE
CORE CORE CORE
CORE CORE CORE
CORE CORE
CORE CORE
CORE

5 Self-Interest, Properly Understood

(pp. 76-78)

During the Founding, there were competing ideas concerning the best way to order the nation's economy. Some, like Alexander Hamilton, thought the natural self-interest of individuals would best serve the nation if exercised in the context of a strong manufacturing and commercial republic. By contrast, Thomas Jefferson saw more value in the self-sufficiency of primarily farming economies. In either case, the Founders relied on free markets – rather than centralized government control – to achieve the goals of economic growth and individual prosperity.

> "The Founders hoped for the general spread of wealth to the majority of Americans. However, they did not believe that government redistribution of wealth was the best way to bring this about."

The Founders hoped for the general spread of wealth to the majority of Americans. However, they did not believe that government redistribution of that wealth was the best way to bring this about. Free markets not only spread more wealth to more people, but also cultivate the civic virtues of industriousness and self-sufficiency and avoid the civic vices of laziness and dependence – vices resulting from the modern paternalistic welfare state.

The modern state trusts the expertise of "objective" bureaucratic central planners to create a strong economy. The Founders, however, thought that individual self-interest channeled through the freedom to contract would best produce sustained economic growth. This freedom to contract depends on government's enforcement of the rule of law, and its upholding the obligations of contracts.

QUESTIONS

1. How did the Founders understand the relationship between the protection of private property and civic virtue?

The Founders believed that allowing individuals to acquire and dispose of property according to their self-interest promoted individual responsibility, industry, and self-sufficiency.

2. What is the key difference between the political economy of the Founders and that of the modern state?

The modern state depends on unelected and unaccountable bureaucrats to regulate and redistribute property among individuals and classes to achieve political ends. By contrast, the Founders thought the opportunities of the free market vastly expanded and most fairly distributed the nation's wealth.

6 The Fire of Opportunity (pp. 79-80)

The protection of property is intended to encourage a flourishing commercial republic. An example is Congress' Article I, Section 8, power to issue patents to inventors and copyrights to authors. Legal protections for patents and copyrights lead to the kind of industry and creativity required for a robust and energetic commercial republic.

QUESTION

1. How does Congress' power to issue patents and copyrights contribute to both civic virtue and the economic success of the commercial republic?

Because government enforces patents and copyrights, inventors and authors have the motivation to use their creative talent and consequently profit from their ideas to the benefit of all.

GO DEEPER

Many people in America question whether a right to private property is just and disagree over the degree to which it should be protected. What do you think? How would the Founders respond to this question?

NOTES:

The Bedrock of the Constitution

In 1783, after the Battle of Yorktown had been won but before the treaty of peace was concluded, General George Washington sent his last report as commander of the Continental Army to the state governors. He observed that Americans were now free and in possession of a great continent rich in "all the necessities and conveniences of life." The potential of the new nation was virtually unlimited, given the times and circumstances of its birth. One could hardly imagine a better beginning.

But then Washington struck a jarring note, "and if their Citizens should not be completely free and happy, *the fault will be entirely their own.*"

With the war won, the hard work of constructing a nation began. What they did now would determine whether the revolution would be seen as a blessing or a curse – not only for present and future generations of Americans but also for the rest of the world, "This is the time of their political probation," Washington continued, "this is the moment when the eyes of the World are turned upon them."

It was eleven years after the Declaration of Independence – and four years after American victory in the Revolutionary War – that a small group of delegates would convene in Philadelphia to create a new charter for governing the new nation. In order to comprehend this historic achievement, we must first understand that this moment and the constitutional document that resulted were built on the great foundational principle of the rule of law.

The rule of law may be the most significant and influential accomplishment of Western constitutional thinking. The very meaning and structure of our Constitution embody this principle. Nowhere expressed, yet evident throughout the Constitution, this bedrock concept is the first principle on which the American legal and political system was built.

THE RULE OF LAW

WE HAVE NOW COMPLETED the discussion of the primary political principles of the Declaration of Independence. Specifically, we covered the principles of equality, natural rights, and the consent of the governed as articulated in the Declaration. We also discussed how the government must protect citizens' natural rights, religious liberty, and private property. Beginning with session five, we look to the legitimate process by which government secures our rights and liberties. In this chapter you will cover with your group the following key concepts:

Key Concepts

1. The rule of law is the fundamental alternative to the arbitrary rule of individuals that often results in despotism and tyranny.

2. The rule of law means that the laws are knowable by all and equally applied to all.

3. A government of laws and not men means that government is limited in its power.

4. The most authoritative and fundamental law is the Constitution; it is the fundamental and supreme law of the land.

5. The ratification of the Articles of Confederation was an important unifying moment for the newly independent American states.

DESPOTISM
A form of absolute rule that uses physical force and deception to control the ruled.

TYRANNY
The combination of all political power in the hands of one person or group.

REPUBLICANISM
A form of government characterized by the rule of law, representative government, and individual liberty required for self government.

6. The Articles of Confederation suffered from structural defects, most notably, the absence of strong executive and judicial departments, leading to legislative abuses of the rights of the people.

7. The Constitutional Convention addressed the weaknesses of the Articles by creating a vigorous, energetic executive department, as well as an independent judiciary.

8. Anti-Federalists criticized the Constitution's strong executive and independent judiciary, citing both as inconsistent with republican principles, but the Federalists successfully passed the republicanism of the Constitution, resulting in unanimous ratification of the document.

The Rule of Law (pp. 82-86)

From antiquity to the present, tyrannical rule has been the preferred governing principle for absolute monarchs and despots. Such rulers have employed both physical force and deception in order to control their subjects. As ancient political philosophers discussed at length, the arbitrary rule of dictators contrasts with the rule of law. The rule of law rests on the idea that the law is superior to any dictate of a particular ruler. Because of their inheritance of British legal traditions, the American colonies had a long experience with the rule of law.

The rule of law requires the laws be known and enforced by independent courts of law. The law should protect all equally, and the magistracy should apply the law to all equally. Government officials must themselves be subject to the law. Indeed, no one is above the law.

The rule of law signifies the inherent limitations of government. Due process requires that the law be applied in an open, fair, and equitable manner. Certain government actions are fundamentally unacceptable, such as issuing punishments without trials, arbitrarily holding or detaining citizens without cause, trying someone for

> "The rule of law rests on the idea that the law is superior to any dictate of a particular ruler."

the same crime more than once, retroactive laws, and the nullification of private contracts.

Finally, the rule of law suggests that of the three governmental powers (making, enforcing, and interpreting the law) lawmaking is central. Particularly important is the most fundamental and authoritative law – the supreme law of the land instituted by the people – the Constitution.

QUESTIONS

1. **What are the four basic features of the American concept of the rule of law?**

   The rule of law consists of the following:

   * open, regular process of law enforcement and due process;

   * equal application of the law to all;

   * government that is limited by certain fundamental principles of justice and equity;

   * subordination of ordinary acts of the legislature to the fundamental law – the Constitution.

EX POST FACTO
Latin for after the fact. Usually in reference to a law that applies retroactively.

2. **What legal actions did the Founders generally understand to be contrary to the first principles of a just and equitable government?**

   Ex post facto laws (retroactive laws), bills of attainder (punishment without trial), double jeopardy (twice being tried for the same crime), and laws impairing the obligation of contracts inherently violated the rule of law.

2 Constitutional Development (pp. 86-89)

In the Middle Ages the idea of a constitution took the form of political agreements between the government and its subjects. The most notable example is England's

Magna Carta of 1215, a document outlining the rights of the people.

The existence of inherent, unalienable, and fundamental rights of the people implies limits to governmental power – that is, government is not free to do anything it wishes. Government must be arranged (i.e. constituted) in order to protect and secure individual rights. A crucial feature of this institutional arrangement is the subordination of the legislative power to law. In other words, there must be an authority higher than the legislative power itself – that authority is the fundamental law.

One of the colonists' principal complaints was that the British Parliament saw itself as sovereign, rather than the law. Britain's lack of a written constitution exacerbated Parliament's view of itself. Instead of a written law, Britain's constitution consisted of past legislative enactments and judicial opinions; there was no single authoritative document upon which the governing authority was based. Such a fundamental document was necessary for the American Founders to bring about a government based upon the rule of law and the sovereignty of the people.

QUESTIONS

1. Why did the American colonists demand a written constitution?

A written constitution that codified both the arrangement of governmental institutions and the limitations of governmental power would better secure the rights of the people.

2. What was the colonists' principal objection to the acts of Parliament leading up to the Revolution?

Their principal objection was Parliament's claim to absolute sovereignty over them without their consent. The colonists thought such a claim to be contrary to the principle of the rule of law.

3 Colonial Experience (pp. 89-91)

British infringement upon the colonists' rights led to the development of state constitutions. Many of these constitutions listed the rights of the people as well as specific limitations on government power. Before the signing of the Declaration of Independence, the colonists drafted and ratified the Articles of Confederation. The Articles formally unified the colonies, establishing a "perpetual union." Although a step in the right direction, the Articles were ultimately insufficient. Foremost among their weaknesses was the lack of an independent executive or judiciary. Although the Articles established some important national legislative powers, it lacked the crucial legislative power of taxation.

The Articles made it difficult to pass simple legislative acts, or to amend the Articles. Such structural defects led to ineffective American foreign policy and serious questions as to the national government's ability to defend itself and enforce its own laws.

QUESTIONS

1. What were the structural defects of the Articles of Confederation?

The Articles suffered from the lack of any legitimate taxing power, the absence of an independent executive to enforce the acts of the national congress, and want of a judiciary power.

4 A Deeper Problem (pp. 91-92)

Government by the people implies majority rule. Though majority rule rightly seems to follow from the "consent of the governed," there is an important problem that invariably surfaces in popular governments – the tyranny of the majority, also known as majority faction. Majority rule can lead to a majority of citizens infringing on the rights of a minority of citizens. Many states experienced this tyranny prior to the Constitutional Convention. Majority factions ruled in most state legislatures precisely because these legislatures lacked effective institutional checks and balances. State executive and judicial departments were weak and could not check unjust legislators. The experience of the Articles demonstrated that popular rule by itself is not sufficient to secure the rights of the people. It is necessary to have a written authoritative fundamental law – a Constitution fit to both secure individual rights and create a government by and for the people.

QUESTIONS

1. **What was the fundamental problem with the legislative supremacy practiced in the states prior to the Constitutional Convention?**

   Because there were no substantial checks on legislative power, majority factions routinely violated the rights and liberties of others and gave special advantage to their own interests.

2. **What is the relationship between the Declaration of Independence and the Constitution?**

   The Declaration generally outlines the inherent rights of the people and the implication of those rights for the purpose of government. The Constitution provides the actual institutional and practical arrangements by which a society seeks to protect the rights of the people.

5 The Constitutional Convention (pp. 92-97)

The weaknesses inherent in the Articles of Confederation led to the calling of the Constitutional Convention in Philadelphia in the summer of 1787. Every state, except one, sent delegates to the Convention to make the constitution "adequate to the exigencies of the union." The greatest statesmen and political minds of generations past and present attended the momentous occasion. Some noteworthy men were absent from the proceeding – those who thought a strong national government to be inconsistent with republicanism; others whose diplomatic duties representing the newly formed union prevented attendance.

The Convention observed two important procedural rules: each state had one vote, and the proceedings were to be confidential. The delegates generally agreed on the principle of separation of powers – that those making the law would neither enforce the law nor interpret and evaluate the law also. In terms of legislative power, serious disagreement arose concerning how representation would be determined. Proponents of the Virginia Plan thought the representatives should be apportioned by a state's population. This, of course, would greatly increase the power of the larger states. Defenders of the New Jersey Plan wanted "one state, one vote" as had been the case with the Articles of Confederation. This "equal" system favored the smaller states, for each small state would be as politically powerful as each large state. The Great Compromise of the Convention resolved this crucial dispute, resulting in proportional representation in the House of Representatives and equal representation in the Senate.

Since this new Constitution was an act of "We the People," popularly elected delegates of each state needed to ratify the document. The new Constitution was not without opposition. Critics of the plan, the Anti-Federalists, thought the Constitution gave too much power to the executive and judicial branches. They also objected to the absence of a Bill of Rights – provisions to protect the people and their rights from the federal government. Ultimately, the supporters of the plan – the Federalists – won. Every state convention voted to ratify the Constitution.

QUESTIONS

1. **What was the major disagreement that led to The Great Compromise? What political principles were at stake in this debate?**

   The disagreement arose concerning apportionment of the legislature. Proponents of the Virginia Plan sought representation according to population, while advocates of the New Jersey Plan sought equal representation – one state, one vote. Representation based on population emphasizes the unity of the country as a single whole and would have been particularly advantageous to states with large commercial cities. Equal representation emphasizes the individual sovereignty of each state and would have favored the smaller states.

2. **What were the Anti-Federalists' concerns?**

   They feared the newly created executive and judicial branches. They thought the executive branch had been given too much power and would develop into a monarchical office. They were also concerned about an independent judiciary, and judges with life tenure on the courts of law.

6 The Momentous Work (pp. 97-98)

The singular moment of the Convention came on September 17, 1787, when the Constitution was read aloud. Although some were skeptical in the beginning, the delegates gained a renewed sense of optimism upon hearing the finished work. Having endured for more than 200 years, the work of the Convention was an unqualified success and a great victory for the proponents of the rule of law and human liberty.

The U.S. Constitution legally confirms the American people as a self-governing nation. It is a profound document accessible to the common sense of the citizens who make it legitimate. The Constitution is the blueprint of our liberty; it defines the rule of law, the structural forms of government, and the limits on the power of that government.

QUESTION

1. **How does the Constitution give U.S. citizens liberty?**

As U.S. citizens, we have liberty because the Constitution defines the rule of law, the structural forms of government, and the limits of power on our government.

GO DEEPER

What is the difference between the rule of law and the rule of men? What are the basic features of the rule of law? How well has our government remained true to the original purpose of making laws?

NOTES: _____

_____

_____

_____

_____

_____

Constituting Liberty

The United States Constitution is quite remarkable. A brief document – only some 5,400 words, handwritten on five pieces of parchment paper – it is characterized by straightforward language that is remarkably accessible. At the same time that it addresses timeless ideas and perennial problems of Western political thought and practice, the Constitution's main concepts are readily accessible.

"Constitutions are not designed for metaphysical or logical subtleties, for niceties of expression, for critical propriety, for elaborate shades of meaning, or for the exercise of philosophical acuteness or judicial research," wrote Joseph Story in the *Commentaries on the Constitution*. "They are instruments of a practical nature, founded on the common business of human life, adapted to common wants, designed for common use, and fitted for common understandings."

Not simply an organizational structure having to do with narrow legal or governmental matters, the Constitution is the arrangement that formally constitutes the American people. It orders our politics, defines our nation, and protects our citizens as a free people.

The challenge was to secure the rights and liberties promised in the Declaration of Independence, preserving a republic that reflected the consent of the governed yet avoided despotism and tyranny. The solution was to create an energetic national government of limited powers, along with the institutions and improvements necessary to make the American experiment work, all carefully enumerated in a written document of fundamental law.

The design, forms, and institutions of the Founders' solution define the necessary conditions of the rule of law and limited government, and hence liberty. That constitutionalism, made up of the various structural concepts embodied in the Constitution of the United States, is one of our most important first principles – not because these concepts are old, or unique, or exclusively ours for that matter, but because they form the architecture of liberty.

CONSTITUTIONALISM
The Architecture of Limited Government

THE CONCEPT OF THE RULE OF LAW, discussed in session five, is the foundation of the structural protections of equal natural rights, the consent of the governed, and limited constitutional government. In session six, we continue the theme of the rule of law and the Constitution. Specifically, we will discuss the idea of constitutionalism established by the articles and amendments of the U.S. Constitution. This will involve discussion about the following key concepts:

Key Concepts

1. The U.S. Constitution embodies the moral and political claims of the Declaration of Independence.

2. The source of power is in the people themselves; the Constitution vests this power in specific governmental institutions.

3. The powers granted by the Constitution are not unlimited.

4. Article I grants specific powers and the means to carry them out to the legislature.

5. The Senate is meant to prevent the passions of the people from having an undue influence upon the legislative process.

6. Article II grants more general executive power to the executive branch.

7. Article III establishes the Supreme Court of the United States, vesting judicial power in it, and in any courts subsequently created by Congress.

8. An independent judiciary judging in agreement with the Constitution is vital to a limited government.

9. The Constitution can be changed, but not easily changed. Since a national consensus must be satisfied, the amendment process of the Constitution is an obstacle to those who would undermine it.

1 The Constitution of the United States (pp. 100-102)

The preamble of the Constitution proclaims "We the People" to be the fundamental authority that establishes the Constitution. It states the government's goals:

- safety and security;

- rule of law, which fosters domestic prosperity;

- establishment of justice, promotion of the general welfare;

- formation of a more perfect Union – all for the sake of securing liberty.

The Founders carefully limited the established government, because they recognized that both too much and too little government threatens liberty.

After the preamble, the Constitution describes the powers and institutions of government. It is divided into seven articles, which are further divided into sections and clauses. The first three articles create three distinct branches of government:

- legislative;

- executive;

- judicial.

The Constitution establishes three coequal branches of government and creates a government of delegated and enumerated powers. That is, the government has only the

"The Founders carefully limited the established government, because they recognized that both too much and too little government threatens liberty."

powers the people give it. The purpose of a constitution is to specify which powers the people grant to the branches of government and what limitations exist upon the exercise and scope of those powers. The Constitution does not grant the federal government unlimited power, rather, it grants particular branches of government a limited set of powers.

QUESTIONS

1. **How does the structure of the government established by the Constitution embody the sovereignty of the people?**

   The people select – directly or indirectly – members of all three branches of government.

2. **How does the Constitution secure liberty for the American people?**

   It creates a limited government dedicated to the rule of law and the protection of natural rights.

2 Article I: The Legislative Power

(pp. 103-105)

The first three articles of the Constitution open with a "Vesting Clause," reiterating that government has no powers beyond what the people delegate to the separate branches. Article I grants specific legislative powers to the Congress. The powers granted are limited in scope, but they are complete within their areas of authority. The grant of power to do something also includes the means to do it. The "necessary and proper" clause is the basis for these implied powers. This clause only grants Congress the authority to make additional laws that are "necessary and proper" for the execution of the powers granted in the Constitution.

VESTING CLAUSE

The clause at the beginning of Articles I-III, denoting which powers and to what extent they are "vested" or granted to a particular branch.

Dividing the legislature into two houses further limits the expansion of legislative power. The House is the more popular chamber, while the Senate (originally) represented the states as individual political entities. Its mode of election, qualifications for office, and longer terms of office are to ensure that the Senate is a more deliberative body, serving as a brake on popular passions.

QUESTIONS

1. What is the importance of the vesting clause?

The vesting clause underscores that the federal government's authority is the result of citizens granting power to particular branches of government.

2. How does the grant of specific powers to Congress maintain the distinction between the state governments and the national government?

A grant of limited and specified powers rather than a general grant of authority allow state and local autonomy in matters that are properly state and local rather than national concerns.

3 Article II: The Executive Power

(pp. 105-107)

After their experience under the British crown, Americans were cautious about executive power. Still, most delegates to the Constitutional Convention understood that a strong executive was necessary. The question they faced was how to devise a strong – but not tyrannical – executive office.

As the chief executive, the president's job is to execute the laws made by Congress. He is also responsible for the enforcement of federal law, and is bound by oath to "preserve, protect and defend the Constitution of the United States." The president has a limited veto power, and can recommend "expedient" measures to the Congress. With the advice and consent of the Senate, he appoints judges and federal offices; he also receives ambassadors and commissions U. S. military officers.

Article II provides a *general* grant of executive power, with the exception of those traditional executive powers (most importantly to declare war) reserved for Congress. The president's law enforcement ability only extends to federal laws. Article II also provides for election by an electoral college, which is intended to encourage the selection of a president who will have a broad and general appeal to a nationwide constituency.

QUESTIONS

1. **How did the Founders respond to the danger of executive tyranny?**

They divided government power into three branches, focused the president on executing the laws made by Congress and granted some executive power to the legislature.

2. **How can the president check the powers of Congress, and vice versa?**

The president can exert a qualified veto to check Congress, and Congress can override a presidential veto, defund executive activities, and impeach the president.

ELECTORAL COLLEGE

The process of election in which each state receives a number of representatives, or electors, who cast votes on behalf of the states for the president.

4 Article III: The Judicial Power

(pp. 107-109)

Article III places the judicial power in a Supreme Court of the United States and any other courts Congress establishes. It does not specify any qualifications for Supreme Court justices. All federal judges are appointed for lifetime terms; their terms expire only in case of death, resignation, or impeachment by the Congress. The Constitution separates the judicial power from the legislative power. The judiciary is a reactive rather than active body. Being vested only with the judicial power, the judiciary is not able to seek out laws to strike down or to change legislative public policy; questions must be brought before the court in actual cases.

> "Being vested only with the judicial power, the judiciary is not able to seek out laws to strike down or to change legislative public policy."

QUESTION

1. Why is it important to insulate the judiciary from the influence of both the executive and the legislative?

The judiciary must be independent of both the executive and legislative branches so they will judge in agreement with the Constitution rather than based on their own interests or political pressures.

5 The Last Articles (pp. 109-111)

Throughout the Constitution, the importance of the states is evident. Article IV requires that "Full Faith and Credit" be granted to the laws and decisions of other states, and that all privileges and immunities of citizenship be granted to residents of every other state. It also provides a mechanism for territories to become states, and a guarantee of republican government to all of the states themselves.

Article V provides the means for amending the Constitution. Amendments may be proposed by two-thirds of both the House and Senate or by two-thirds of the states calling for a constitutional convention. The proposal must then be ratified by three-fourths of the states.

Article VII provides that the Constitution must be ratified by state conventions rather than legislatures.

QUESTIONS

1. **What is the meaning and importance of the Full Faith and Credit Clause?**

   The Full Faith and Credit Clause of Article IV of the U.S. Constitution requires each state to respect and give "full faith and credit" to the decisions and laws of all other states, and ensures the legal basis for common citizenship.

2. **Why is the Constitution's amendment process, as laid out in Article V, essential for the existence of the United States as a limited constitutional republic?**

   The amendment process makes it very hard to change the Constitution based on immediate passions or political whim. At the same time, it allows constitutional change by the people, thereby strengthening the authority of the Constitution and underscoring popular sovereignty as a basis for the American Republic.

6 A Bill of Rights (pp. 111-114)

The Bill of Rights, proposed and ratified by the states in 1791, comprises the first 10 amendments to the Constitution.

The First and Second Amendments guarantee substantive rights – religious liberty, freedom of speech, assembly and petition, and the right to keep and bear arms. The next six are procedural amendments, largely concerned with criminal due process, aimed at preventing arbitrary executive authority: warrants require probable cause; someone cannot be tried twice for the same crime or be forced to incriminate himself; the accused have a right to speedy, public trial and the assistance of counsel; and criminal cases require juries. The Ninth and Tenth Amendments reiterate the basic theory that undergirds the Constitution: government exists to preserve rights that stem from the people themselves, and the powers of

PROBABLE CAUSE

The reasonable belief that a crime has been or will be committed. The standard of proof required for a warrant.

the national government are limited to those granted in the Constitution itself. All other governmental powers are reserved to the states or to the people themselves.

These amendments were generally understood to apply to the federal government only, and not as specific prohibitions of state action. Until 1925, the Supreme Court upheld that view; since then, the doctrine of "incorporation" has interpreted the Bill of Rights as a restraint upon state governments.

QUESTIONS

1. What is the doctrine of "incorporation?

The doctrine of "incorporation" extends the Bill of Rights to the states, while previously it was held to be a limit on federal authority only.

2. What is the significance of the Ninth and Tenth Amendments?

The last two amendments to the Bill of Rights reinforced the political and philosophical principles of the Founding: that the federal government exists solely due to the will of the people and the constitutive state, and cannot exercise any powers not delegated to it specifically by the states or the people.

7 Amendments to the Constitution

(pp. 114-115)

Although many have been proposed, only 27 amendments have passed:

- Eleventh: limits court jurisdiction with regard to suits against the states;

- Twelfth: requires separate balloting for president and vice-president;

> "The powers of the national government are limited to those granted in the Constitution itself. All other governmental powers are reserved to the states or to the people themselves."

> "The federal government exists solely due to the will of the people and the constitutive state, and cannot exercise any powers not delegated to it specifically by the states or the people."

- Thirteenth-Fifteenth: the Civil War Amendments abolish slavery, confer citizenship on all persons born or naturalized in the United States, and prohibit the states from violating the privileges or immunities of citizenship, the due process of law, or the equal protection of the law;

- Fifteenth: protects voting rights regardless of race, color, or former enslavement;

- Sixteenth: gave Congress the power to tax incomes;

- Seventeenth: mandates direct election of senators;

- Eighteenth, Twenty-First: prohibited the manufacture, sale, or transport of intoxicating liquors; repealed by the Twenty-First Amendment;

- Nineteenth: guarantees women the right to vote;

- Twentieth: reduces the amount of time between the national election and the inauguration;

- Twenty-Second: limits the presidency to two four-year terms of office;

- Twenty-Third: grants electors to Washington, D.C.;

- Twenty-Fourth: abolishes the use of poll taxes in federal elections;

- Twenty-Fifth: standardizes the line of presidential succession;

- Twenty-Sixth: lowers the voting age from 21 to 18;

- Twenty-Seventh: provides that Congressional pay raises do not take effect until there has been another election.

QUESTIONS

1. How are many of the amendments related to specific issues?

Many amendments are responses to problems that presented themselves to the country, such as the Civil War amendments, which dealt with certain issues that arose in the aftermath of the war.

2. How do the Progressive-era amendments represent an increase in governmental power and a change in the practice of federalism?

The Sixteenth Amendment increases the power of the federal government by creating a progressive tax on personal income. The Seventeenth Amendment weakens the states in relation to the federal government by making Senators elected rather than appointed by state legislatures.

GO DEEPER

Today people often speak about our government's inefficiencies — that government has become too big and clumsy. How well does our current system of government reflect the structure outlined by the Founders in the Constitution? Have we lost something by straying from this original structure? And which do you think has more merit: our current system or the one outlined by the Constitution?

NOTES:

SESSION 6

Constitutionalism:
The Architecture
of Limited
Government

Auxiliary Precautions

It is important to understand how the workings of the Constitution relate to the principles underlying it.

"A dependence on the people is, no doubt, the primary control on the government," Madison noted in *Federalist* 51, "but experience has taught mankind the necessity of auxiliary precautions." The Founders believed that citizen virtue was crucial for the success of republican government, but they also knew that passion and interest were permanent parts of human nature. Rather than relying on a predominance of virtue, the Founders designed a system that would harness man's competing interests — not to lower politics to questions of narrow self-interest but to provide what they called "the defect of better motives."

So in addition to the formal provisions of the document, three important but unstated mechanisms at work in the Constitution demand our attention: the extended republic, the separation of powers, and federalism. These "auxiliary precautions" constitute improvements in the science of politics developed by the Founders and form the basis of what they considered "a republican remedy for the diseases most incident to republican government." They are crucial to the operational success of our constitutional system.

Two other monumental issues of constitutional meaning — both of which are widely misunderstood today — are crucial to understanding the principles of constitutionalism in practice: who in the end says what the Constitution means? And how are we to understand the Constitution's compromises with slavery? The answers to these questions, as well as the extent to which the workings of the constitutional government are consistent with the principles of liberty, will go far in establishing our fidelity to the American Constitution.

CONSTITUTIONALISM IN PRACTICE

The Workings of Ordered Liberty

IN SESSION SIX, we examined the rule of law, the idea of constitutionalism, and the outline of the U.S. Constitution. We discussed the three branches of government and their enumerated limited powers. Session seven continues on the theme of government's design. We will explore the particular structure of our Constitution, with its separation of powers, federalism, and checks and balances. To understand these structures, think about the following key concepts:

Key Concepts

1. The most serious danger of a society where the people are sovereign is majority tyranny – the creation of unjust laws by the majority that violate the rights of the minority.

2. In our republican government the people elect individuals to exercise the functions of government.

3. The separation of the legislative, executive, and judicial branches is essential to prevent tyranny.

4. The Constitution separates the powers of government so that each branch may effectively hold accountable the activities of the other branches.

5. The Constitution divides the tasks of government between the federal and state governments. Judicial review of legislative and executive action is essential to preventing legislative and executive abuse.

6. Judicial authority extends only to the explicit requirements and restrictions stated in the Constitution.

7. Each branch of government has the right and duty to interpret and uphold the Constitution. While the meaning of the Constitution is fixed and permanent, no branch of government has the final say on what the Constitution means.

1 Representation and the Extended Republic (pp. 118-119)

The United States is a republic. An essential feature of our republicanism is representation. People exercise their consent by electing representatives who make the laws and policies for the nation. So long as the lawmakers remain accountable to the people through frequent and fair elections, the people remain "sovereign" over lawmaking.

Representation is preferable to direct democracy for at least two reasons:

- It increases the likelihood that laws and policies will be formulated in a productive and reflective way. Requiring or permitting every citizen to vote on every law and policy (as would be required in a pure democracy) is impractical given the large size of our nation. A smaller group of popularly chosen individuals who reflect their constituents' views is more practical.

- Representation reduces the chance that bad laws will be passed. Representation limits the effects of majority factions. Placing the lawmaking duties in the hands of individuals who encompass a wide array of opinions and interests lessens the likelihood of a tyranny of the majority.

REPUBLIC
A form of government characterized by the rule of law, representative government, and individual liberty.

78

1. **How does representation combat the development and operation of majority faction?**

Representation embodies the opinions of the community but allows selected individuals to make law for the community. Elections are intended to make representatives responsive to majority opinion rather than narrow special interests harmful to the common good.

2. **What is the distinction between a republic and a pure democracy?**

A democracy consists of a small community of individuals, each of whom votes directly for each law and policy of the society. A republic places the legislative functions in the hands of a select group of individuals, each of whom is elected to office by the people.

> "Representation reduces the chance that bad laws will be passed."

The Separation of Powers (pp. 119-122)

The Constitution separates the power of government into three distinct branches:

- Legislative, embodied in Congress;
- Executive, embodied in the president;
- Judicial, embodied in the Supreme Court and other federal courts.

No person or persons may serve in any two branches of government simultaneously. Distributing these powers among different individuals avoids the concentration of power that often leads to tyranny.

The Constitution incorporates a degree of power-sharing among the departments so as to foster cooperation and accountability – veto power of the executive over legislation, advice and consent power of the legislature over executive and judicial appointments, and judicial review of legislative and executive action.

QUESTIONS

1. What danger is avoided by distributing the legislative, executive, and judicial power among different individuals?

The separating of these powers prevents the accumulation of all government power into the hands of a single individual or body of individuals.

2. What are some positive aspects of the division of government power?

The mutual accountability each branch exercises upon the other two as well, as the various ways in which the branches share particular governmental duties, results in better legislation, better administration and enforcement of the laws, and better judicial rulings.

3 Federalism: A Nation of States

(pp. 122-124)

The United States is a compound republic composed of two distinct levels of government:

- a national or federal government;
- multiple state governments.

The institutional relationship and distribution of powers between the states and the federal government is known as "federalism." Federalism intends to bring about two political goods:

- a strong national government able to defend the nation and serve the national economy;
- a multiplicity of state governments responsible for those things that regularly concern the lives, liberty, and property of the people (e.g. health, safety, and morals of the people).

In contrast to today, the Founders did not intend the federal government to be the primary controller of

"In contrast to today, the Founders did not intend the federal government to be the primary controller of people's lives."

people's lives. Since the federal government's power is restricted to that granted to particular branches in the Constitution, powers not granted were to be reserved to the states, or to the people. In other words, if the Constitution is silent concerning a particular area of government, then that area falls within the jurisdiction of each state, not the national government.

QUESTION

1. **According to the Framers of the Constitution, what is the proper scope of the federal government's power?**

The extent of the federal government is limited to those powers delegated to the particular branches of the government in the Constitution. All other powers are reserved to the states or the people.

Judicial Review (pp. 124-126)

By creating an independent judicial branch, the Founders sought an objective body to settle legal disputes. When a case arises within the jurisdiction of the federal courts, it is the duty of judges to evaluate any laws passed in Congress or any executive actions at issue in the particular case. These legislative and executive acts are to be measured against the requirements and restrictions within the Constitution. If a case arises in which an act is determined to be inconsistent with some part of the Constitution, it is the duty of the courts to void the act. The power to make such declarations in particular cases is called "judicial review." Judicial review of the activities of the political branches safeguards the rights of individuals against legislative and executive branches seizing power.

Legal claims concerning rights must be distinguished from political questions concerning public policy and the common good. The court only has the authority to speak to the former. The court is not empowered to substitute its own policy preferences for that of the

JUDICIAL REVIEW

The power to determine the consistency of particular acts with the Constitution.

"The court is not empowered to substitute its own policy preferences for that of the legislature."

81

legislature. If Congress passes a law within the scope of its constitutional authority, and if this law does not violate any of the requirements or restrictions in the Constitution, then the courts do not have the authority to strike down such a law. Even if the judges believe the law to be unwise or ineffective public policy, they still must not overturn the law. The making and enforcing of public policy belongs to the elected representatives in the Congress and Executive branches. Judges must exercise restraint and not make rulings on political (or public policy) grounds.

QUESTION

1. **What is the significance of the distinction between political questions and legal questions?**

Legal questions reviewable by the judiciary arise when the political branches overstep their constitutional authority – exercising powers not granted, violating the protected rights of individuals. Political decisions concerning public policy and the common good, while they must agree with the Constitution, are to be left to the political branches of government.

JURISPRUDENCE

An understanding of law, the legal process, and the application of the law in particular circumstances.

5 Who Says What the Constitution Means? (pp. 127-130)

The judiciary is often identified as the chief interpreter of the Constitution. This is incorrect. To be sure, the judiciary's role in constitutional interpretation is important. Supreme Court rulings in particular cases often become precedents for future rulings in similar cases. Furthermore, the court's longstanding jurisprudence on specific constitutional questions often guides legislators and executives in the course of their lawmaking and law enforcement.

The Supreme Court's interpretations of the Constitution are authoritative and final only with respect to the particular case before the court. When the court addresses questions and issues beyond the scope of the case before them, their rendering of the Constitution is no more legally authoritative than those of the legislature and the executive.

The members of all three branches of government must be diligent and careful interpreters of the Constitution. Each branch has a duty to uphold the Constitution as the supreme law of the land. Congress should only pass laws it believes are constitutional; the president should only sign laws thought to be constitutional; the judiciary should only uphold laws it judges to be constitutional. In other words, no branch of government is the exclusive interpreter of the Constitution. In order for the separation of powers to properly function, each branch must take its duty to uphold the Constitution seriously.

"No branch of government is the exclusive interpreter of the Constitution."

QUESTIONS

1. **Among the three branches of government, which is the exclusive interpreter of the Constitution?**

   No branch of government can claim an exclusive right or authority to interpret the Constitution because each branch, in the exercise of its authority, interprets the Constitution. This is called coordinate branch construction.

2. **Among the branches of government, which has the final say on the meaning of the Constitution?**

   None of the three branches have "final" say on the Constitution's meaning. Although Supreme Court decisions are final in particular cases, general statements and interpretations of the court beyond those decisions are not final and have regularly been revised or reversed by later rulings. Furthermore, Congress retains the authority to set the jurisdiction of the courts; that is to say, Congress controls the sorts of cases the court may decide.

6 A Bundle of Compromises: Slavery Revisited (pp. 130-134)

Although it never uses the terms "slave" or "slavery," and always refers to "persons," the Constitution contains three clauses dealing with the institution of slavery. These compromises were necessary at the Convention to secure unified support for the Constitution. The first concerned the counting of slaves for the purpose of representation and taxation in Congress. The Convention decided to count the whole number of free persons but only "three-fifths of all other persons (i.e. the slave population), an abolitionist proposal intended to diminish the political power of the slaveholding states.

The second clause concerned the existence of the slave trade. The Constitution prohibited Congress from outlawing the slave trade before 1808. Congress eliminated the international slave trade in 1808.

The third clause involved the return of fugitive slaves to their owners. The Constitution required the return of those persons "held to service or labor in one state, under the laws thereof." The language of this clause indicates that slavery was only legitimate in particular states and had no federal status.

Although the Constitution did not immediately eradicate the institution of slavery, it is significant that the Constitution not only refrained from any endorsement of slavery, but also pointed toward the fundamental injustice of slavery – an injustice that would be constitutionally remedied with ratification of the Thirteenth, Fourteenth and Fifteenth Amendments.

QUESTIONS

1. **How do the Founders' original compromises with slavery indicate their understanding of the fundamental injustice of slavery and reveal their desire to eliminate the institution?**

By refusing to count the full number of slaves held to service in the states, the Founders designed the Three-Fifths Compromise to limit the political power of pro-slavery interests. The explicit prohibition of any congressional law banning the slave trade before 1808 recognized Congress' power to ban the trade after 1808, which they did. The language of the fugitive slave clause recognizes slaves as persons and refuses to recognize the practice of slavery as either legal or just.

2. **Why didn't the Founders simply end slavery at the Constitutional Convention?**

Although the Founders recognized the fundamental inconsistency between the existence of slavery and the natural rights of all human beings, the political history of some states had resulted in their interests being tied to the continuation of slavery. The compromises concerning slavery in the Constitution were essential to its passage, and thus the creation of an incomplete framework for eradicating slavery and for expanding liberty and equality for all.

Constitutional Fidelity (p. 134)

The Constitution is the fundamental act of the people. Because the people are sovereign, the Constitution stands as the supreme law of the land – supreme over the will of the legislative, executive, and judicial branches. In order to perform their jobs well and authoritatively, those elected or appointed to government office must remain faithful to the requirements and responsibilities of the Constitution.

QUESTION

1. **What does fidelity to the Constitution require from those who govern?**

Fidelity to the Constitution requires taking seriously and obeying the limitations and demands of the Constitution.

"Because the people are sovereign, the Constitution stands as the supreme law of the land – supreme over the will of the legislative, executive, and judicial branches."

Government officials must make an effort to discern the meaning of the Constitution (as its authors understood it) and to abide by the Constitution's parameters faithfully.

GO DEEPER

The view of government as an organization that exists to "do" certain things for its citizens and to promote what is best for the general welfare is prevalent. After studying the different elements of the Constitution, do you think that this is the purpose the Founders intended government to serve? Is a government that provides benefits for its people consistent with our Founding principles?

NOTES:

Governing Ourselves

Levi Preston of Danvers, Massachusetts, was in his early twenties in the spring of 1775 when he fought at the Battle of Concord.

Many years later, Captain Preston was asked why he went to fight that day. Was it the intolerable oppressions of British colonial policy, or the Stamp Act? "I never saw any stamps." What about the tax on tea? "I never drank a drop of the stuff; the boys threw it all overboard." It must have been all your reading of Harrington, Sidney, and Locke on the principles of liberty? "Never heard of 'em. We read only the Bible, the catechism, Watt's *Psalms and Hymns*, and the *Almanack*." Well, what was it? asked the interviewer. "Young man, what we meant in going for those redcoats was this: we always had governed ourselves, and we always meant to. They didn't mean we should."

The Founders understood self-government in the twofold sense of *political* self-government, in which we govern ourselves as a political community, and of *moral* self-government, according to which each individual is responsible for governing himself. Individuals could not govern themselves as a body politic unless they were each first capable of governing themselves as individuals, families, and communities.

The purpose of limiting government, assuring rights, and guaranteeing the consent of the governed is to protect a vast realm of human freedom. That freedom creates a great space for the primary institutions of civil society – family, school, church, and private associations – to flourish, forming the habits and virtues required for liberty. It was through these institutions that man secured, as it says in the Constitution, "the blessings of liberty." Moral self-government both precedes and completes political self-government, and thus political freedom. It is in this sense that the primary as well as the culminating first principle of American liberty is self-government.

THE VIRTUES OF SELF-GOVERNMENT

Building Community, Forming Character, and Making Citizens

S O FAR WE HAVE COVERED the foundational principles of liberty found in the Declaration of Independence and the core rights of religious liberty and private property. Then we looked at the rule of law and constitutional structure of government needed to uphold these principles. In this session, we will continue to discuss the structures needed to preserve the principles of government, focusing on the virtues and moral character necessary for free government and to maintain a republican constitutional order. Session eight leads you to think about these key concepts:

Key Concepts

1. Moral formation is vital for the maintenance of self-government. If the moral character of the people fails, so, too, will the republican character of the government.

2. Political self-government requires moral self-government. Moral self-government is the result of upbringing and education.

3. The Founders emphasized self-reliance, hard work, courage, knowledge of the natural rights tradition, and moderation in the people.

4. The Founders recognized the function of religion in forming morals. Regardless of their theological differences, they understood that a free people required religion.

5. The Founders knew education must have a moral component as well as a civic component. So, they promoted the study of the principles that founded America, with emphasis on natural law and natural rights.

6. Society has an interest in promoting the family and stable marriages, because these are the most intimate private associations and the source of private morality.

Two Kinds of Self-Government

(pp. 135-136)

VIRTUE
Quality of character relating to moral excellence.

When we consider self-government today, we usually think of political participation and institutions. The Founders, too, linked self-government with these, but also recognized that certain preconditions were necessary as well. Political self-government as a community requires moral self-government as an individual. So the Founders were concerned with the civic virtues that formed the foundation of the activities and institutions associated with self-government. Because forming the right moral character is a constant challenge, the American project remains an experiment.

"Because forming the right moral character is a constant challenge, the American project remains an experiment."

The family, schools, churches, and private associations — the primary institutions of society — develop the virtues appropriate for self-government. The autonomy of these primary institutions creates the moral self-government required for political self-government. Moral self-government is both the precondition for, and end-result of, political self-government.

1. **What is the link between moral virtue and the civic virtues necessary for the maintenance of a free society?**

People cannot be expected to govern themselves as a political community if individual members do not have the moral capacity to govern themselves morally.

2 The Challenge of Self-Government

(pp. 136-139)

American liberty is inseparable from the Founders' understanding of virtue. Liberty is the moral use of freedom. It is not the morally unrestrained pursuit of any objects of one's passions. Indecent behavior, not conforming to rules and morals of society, is incompatible with reason and morality. Likewise, liberty agrees with man's higher nature – his rational and morally responsible nature. When a man becomes a slave to his passions, he has given up his rationality – and his liberty.

The Founders recognized both the depravity to which a man could sink and the heights to which he might rise, so they designed the institutions of government in light of human nature. Virtue was necessary, but to rely on virtue alone would be insufficient to protect liberty. Limited constitutional government is only possible when people have good moral character. If that moral character were unattainable, the cause of republican government would be doomed from the start. John Adams wrote, the Constitution "was made only for a moral and religious people."

> "Limited constitutional government is only possible when the people have good moral character."

QUESTIONS

1. **What is the connection between liberty, reason, and moral responsibility?**

Reason is what allows human beings to be morally responsible. Liberty is the freedom of a rational and morally responsible person.

2. How does the Constitution itself respond to the fact that human beings are imperfect?

The Founders knew men were capable of virtue, but also knew that virtuous statesmen would not always be in charge. They designed government to operate and check it without relying on the motives of individuals.

American Virtues (pp. 139-142)

The Founders' writings emphasized the four following types of civic virtue:

- Self-reliance: Hard work, both physical and intellectual, was encouraged to form moral character. Churches, family, and community formed such an independent character. Piety and patriotism demanded private charity. An independent character felt shame about receiving welfare, and saw government welfare was a last resort only for those who had nowhere else to turn. Though welfare may be necessary, a good character demands that it be temporary and eventually repaid.

- Courage: James Madison called courage the "vigilant and manly spirit which actuates the people of America, a spirit which nourishes freedom." Courage is necessary to confront foreign and domestic threats. Courageous people have the strength to stand against the advance of despotism. The Founders promoted the morality of risk and reward, discipline and skill, prudence and justice.

- Responsibility: Citizens must understand that not all exercises of authority are despotic; some duties will be burdensome yet still legitimate. People should be able

STEWARDSHIP
Responsible management of one's affairs or property.

DESPOTISM
A form of absolute rule that uses physical force and deception to control the ruled.

to distinguish liberty from license. Citizens need to know the natural rights principles of the Declaration of Independence and have the capacity to be morally responsible people.

- Personal and public moderation: Moral people must rule over their passions rather than submit to them, and respect the rights of others, the constitutional process, and the rule of law. They promote prudence, justice, wisdom, moderation, courage, hope, and charity. A society ruled by a limited constitution would reinforce these virtues just as they, in turn, would reinforce the limited character of government.

QUESTIONS

1. What did John Adams identify as required for a free society?

John Adams argued that only religious and moral people could maintain a free society.

2. How do habits of dependency, such as welfare, undermine the virtues required for limited government?

Dependency destroys the jealous stewardship of liberty and the sense of self-reliance that is critical for keeping citizens independent and government restrained.

4

Constitutional Morality (pp. 143-146)

The morality of a people is inseparable from its form of government. Under the Articles of Confederation, state governments had been dominated by petty politics, political passions, and special interests, which encouraged a petty and jealous character in the people. Thus, the Constitution of 1787 was a step toward moral reform as well as political reform. Good laws encourage good character, which in turn, promotes good government. All

"Good laws encourage good character, which in turn promotes good government."

laws legislate morality by promoting or prohibiting certain behavior; laws shape its citizens' character.

Federal power was limited in order to maintain the very liberty it was meant to support. State and local governments held the primary responsibility for promoting moral character. While the federal government has certain *delegated* and *enumerated* powers, the state constitutions retain the authority to employ police powers (sometimes called reserved powers), which went beyond law enforcement to include legislating for the health, safety, welfare, education, and morality of state residents.

QUESTIONS

1. What is the link between public morality and the form of government?

The morality of a people indicates the degree of government they will tolerate: an immoral people pursuing pleasure at all costs will give up more freedom than a virtuous people interested in maintaining their self-government.

2. How does a limited constitutional government promote the moral character it requires?

Limiting governmental power and enabling greater independence in the states promotes self-reliance in the people.

5 Liberty and Learning (pp. 147-149)

The Founders believed that promoting education was the best defense against tyranny. The Founders' rightly saw education as a means of teaching virtue and, therefore, shaping the character of the citizens. John Adams, Thomas Jefferson, and James Madison all recognized the importance of a primary education that emphasized morality, republican virtue, and the principles of liberty, in addition to studying traditional subjects. Colleges would expand on this education while still instilling the

"The Founders believed that promoting education was the best defense against tyranny."

"precepts of virtue and order." Even law schools would include a moral component. Jefferson and Madison proposed a course for the University of Virginia's law school that required reading Locke, the Declaration of Independence, the *Federalist Papers,* legislative acts from the state, and Washington's Farewell Address. Education was intended to promote useful knowledge, teach general liberal arts, and instill the rights and duties of citizenship; all are vital to a free people.

QUESTIONS

1. What is the relationship between republican government and moral education?

A republic depends on the moral character of the citizens. Therefore, a republic cannot survive if it is unconcerned with the education of its citizens. The U.S. Republic depends on understanding and committing to certain political principles.

2. Why is it important for lawyers in particular to be educated in natural rights and morality?

In a republic, an education in the natural rights tradition and the natural law theory of the Founding is vital for lawyers. This is because lawyers will be involved in interpreting and applying the laws derived from these principles. Those who practice the law must know both the law as well as the principled justification for the law.

Enlightened Patriotism (pp. 149-151)

Education in a democratic republic must include the development of an enlightened patriotism. Public deliberation requires public education and a common language. The formation of good citizens was not limited to those born in the United States. American identity is based on principles rather than ethnicity or national

NATURALIZATION
The legal process of becoming a citizen.

origin. The process of naturalization of immigrants seeks to replace foreign loyalties and philosophies with a loyalty to the American constitutional order. Thus, the naturalization process involves an oath to the Constitution and an education in the history, theory, and institutions of the United States.

QUESTIONS

1. Why is a common language important in the United States?

Free government requires popular deliberation and that requires a commonly shared language, which in the United States is English.

2. How does the naturalization process accord with the principles of the Founding?

The United States is a nation based on ideas rather than on ethnicity or tradition. These principles of liberty are true, despite any other ethnic or national differences. As a result, anyone who agrees with and accepts these principles can, in theory, go through the process of becoming a naturalized American citizen.

7 The Institutions of Civil Society

(pp. 151-154)

The Founders knew that republican government required a certain moral character from its citizens. The laws, by themselves, were insufficient. The Founders saw the moral character of individual lawmakers as the "surest pledges" of prudent counsel and saw in "the pure and immutable principles of private morality" the foundations for American policy. Public policy depends on private moral character. Non-governmental institutions, such as the family, religion, and private associations, must operate where government cannot. The primary institutions of civil society transform selfish and solitary individuals into morally responsible citizens, and thereby strengthen republican government.

In the early period of the American republic, government provided only a minimal safety net. The solution to poverty was not massive welfare systems, but education, work, religion, and the family – the institutions of civil society. Local government cared for the truly destitute, but encouraged private associations to provide mutual aid and charity. Decentralized political life encourages people to unite into private associations, which in turn reinforce the virtues necessary for republican government.

QUESTIONS

1. **Why is the family important for American political life?**

The family is the first and primary shaper and educator of character and morality. Other institutions of civil society, such as in religion and the schools, aide the family in providing for moral formation.

2. **Why did the Founders reject massive, centralized welfare programs?**

Such programs foster habits of dependency in the recipient and apathy toward those in need among the rest of the citizenry. With charity as a mostly private affair, the people become more self-reliant and take an active interest in those less fortunate.

8 Religion and Republican Government (pp. 154-156)

Civil society stems from personal relations and the public associations – especially religion – that manifest our deepest convictions. Religion and morality lead to political prosperity. It is possible that some will have a morality that does not depend upon religion, but such individuals are the exception to the rule. Because religion promotes virtue, it is a component of civic education. Schools, after all, are "nurseries of wise and good men." Education grounded on morality and recognition of religious faith forms the moral character that self-government requires.

QUESTION

1. Why is a moral education appropriate in a self-governing republic?

Religion and morality teach the moral beliefs that are required for republican government. Since only a few will be able to deduce these principles from reason alone, a moral component grounded in religious faith a necessary part of education – provided, of course, that the religion in question promotes the moral virtues required for free government.

Family and the Founders (pp. 156-158)

Though rarely addressed at the time, the family was understood to be the first pre-political institution in civil society. It is the first teacher of morality, and it is the critical link between private moral virtue and public civic virtue. Understanding the importance of private morality for public policy, the Founders saw the family as the pre-condition of civil society and public morality. State and local laws, therefore, supported marriage, family, and parental authority.

"Though rarely addressed at the time, the family was understood to be the first pre-political institution in civil society."

QUESTION

1. Why is the family important for free government?

The family is the center of a future citizen's moral and social education, and so the formation of good character, both private and public, is vital for free government.

10 A Republic, If You Can Keep It

(pp. 159-160)

The Founders knew that republican government ultimately depends on the character of the people: if the people lack virtue, they would soon lose their freedom. Self-government relies on personal and political virtues directed toward self-reliance, public spiritedness, civic knowledge, and personal and public moderation.

QUESTION

1. **Why must a republican government promote virtue and education?**

Republican government depends on the capacity of the people to govern themselves. In a republic, public leaders will reflect the moral character of the people.

GO DEEPER

After reading this session on self-government, do you think that we still live in a virtuous society? Are the characteristics necessary for self-government still present in our general population? Give examples. What does this mean for self-government today?

NOTES:

SESSION 8

The Virtues of
Self-Government:
Building Com-
munity, Forming
Character, and
Making Citizens

Independence Forever

Independence was the clarion call of the American Revolution.

Independence Day is our greatest national celebration, with barbecues, parades, speeches, and fireworks all across the country. And although there seem to be fewer grand commemorations these days, historically the Fourth of July has been the occasion for solemn ceremonies and great speeches about the meaning and purpose of America. That's because, while we tend to think of independence mainly as an important historic event that marks our separation from Great Britain, the Founders and subsequent generations had a larger understanding of what was signified by the national independence they were celebrating.

Americans sought independence not only from Great Britain, after all, but also from military occupation, royal overseers, arbitrary laws, taxation without representation, and — as it says in the Declaration of Independence — everything that "evinces a design to reduce them under absolute Despotism." But in doing so they also were declaring their unity — or interdependence — as a people, a compact of states, and a new nation. Independence implied at the same time *separation* as well as the creation of a new and independent country, living and governing by its own means and according to its own ways.

The concept of independence — that is, what we mean when we speak of American independence — has profound implications for how we understand and govern ourselves as a nation, and how we justify and defend ourselves as an independent actor on the world stage. Properly understood, independence takes on a much more compelling meaning, then and now, and is a first principle of American liberty.

THE COMMAND OF OUR FORTUNES

Sovereign Independence and America's Role in the World

IN THE PREVIOUS SESSIONS, we talked about the principles of the American Founding, the constitutional government that secures those principles, and the public and private character needed for republican self-government. We turn now to what these principles mean for foreign policy and America's relationship with other nations. Session nine presents what our Founding principles mean in the context of U.S. defense and foreign policy. As we think about America's role in the world, keep in mind the following key concepts:

Key Concepts

1. Foreign policy decisions ought to be informed by prudence, which is the application of general principles to particular circumstances.

2. A self-sufficient government is not only free from foreign control or dominance, but also effectively maintains both internal and external security.

3. Protecting the people from external threats is part of the duty of government to secure the right of the people to self-preservation.

4. National security includes not only military force, but also use of non-military means, such as diplomacy, treaties, and international trade.

5. U.S. security and economic interests are legitimate factors when weighing foreign policy decisions.

6. International trade should be conducted with justice and benevolence, or kindness. The United States should enter into agreements in good faith and should fulfill its treaty obligations.

7. U.S. foreign policy should be concerned with the lasting preservation of American independence.

1 A Separate and Equal Station (pp. 162-165)

"A nation is sovereign if it controls its own internal affairs and enjoys status and recognition as an independent nation among other nations."

The language of the Declaration of Independence reveals a great deal about the nature of "independence." Establishing America's right to assume a "separate and equal" station among the world powers likewise establishes America's status as a sovereign nation. A nation is sovereign if it controls its own internal affairs and enjoys a status and recognition as an independent nation among other nations. The Declaration also justified America's decision to separate from Britain. The justification of separation implies America's status as a sovereign self-governing nation — equal in rank to other nations.

QUESTION

1. How is America a *particular* nation? How does the particularity of America relate to its universal principles in the area of foreign policy?

America is a particular nation with unique geographic, historical, and social circumstances and conditions. The task of foreign policy is to uphold the universal principles America is based on in ways that meet the practical challenges and requirements of international politics.

Prudence and Foreign Affairs (pp. 165-168)

Distinct political communities differ in history, geography, and, most importantly, opinions of justice and government. These natural differences result in conflicts between and among nations. Foreign policy describes the ways in which nations choose to deal with each other. The Founders rejected both the notion of idealism and of realism in foreign policy because idealism tends to result in inflexible moral principles to the exclusion of practical political necessities and realism focuses on power to the exclusion of any moral principle. The Founders thought prudence – the application of principles to a particular circumstance – should shape foreign policy decisions.

QUESTION

1. How can the Founders' reputed "isolationism" in foreign policy be better understood as a prudent foreign policy decision?

After establishing its independence, America was a weak and vulnerable nation. This required that America avoid European wars and entanglements while it strengthened its national security, established institutions of government, and improved its national economy.

The Command of Our Fortunes: Sovereign Independence and America's Role in the World

"Prudence – the application of principles to a particular circumstance – should shape foreign policy decisions."

3 The Command of Our Own Fortunes (pp. 168-170)

Although key Founders disagreed about particular foreign policy choices in the early republic, they broadly agreed on the general principles and purposes that ought to govern American foreign policy: maintaining America's national independence and securing the nation's long-term safety and happiness.

President George Washington advocated neutrality in European wars. His position was not out of an idealistic commitment to non-intervention or pacifism, but as a prudent response to American's geographical and military situation in the 1780s. America's physical isolation from the European continent allowed the United States to strengthen its military while cementing its newly formed constitutional institutions.

Self-sufficiency is a necessary condition for true independence. A self-sufficient republican government implies:

- freedom from the control or dominance of any foreign power;

- the ability to choose its own leaders through frequent and fair elections;

- the ability to pass its own laws;

- the ability to maintain both internal and external security.

QUESTION

1. **Given the well-known disagreements during the Washington administration concerning particular foreign policies, in what sense is there a unified view of foreign policy at the time of the Founding?**

Individuals such as Alexander Hamilton and Thomas Jefferson disagreed on how to bring about the common goal of a secure and stable America. Hamilton strongly favored building up American military strength first whereas

Jefferson favored diplomacy more. But both men believed in an independent and sovereign America.

4 Safety and Happiness (pp. 170-174)

The primary purpose of national security is to protect the United States from external threats. Safety, in the most fundamental sense, secures our natural right to self-preservation. Our ability to enjoy the blessings of liberty depends upon the ability of government to keep us safe. National security is not limited to the use of military force; it includes diplomacy, international commerce, and political alliances. Yet, a strong, well-funded, well-trained military ready to defend our country at any time is of critical importance. National sovereignty includes not only the right to defend ourselves from attack, but also the right to eliminate threats before they strike. While the preservation of our rights and liberties is fundamental, circumstances may sometimes require sacrifices on the part of the American people in order to maintain our safety and security for the sake of those rights and liberties. It is the highest duty of the national government, and a core responsibility assigned by the Constitution, to provide for the national defense.

"National security is not limited to the use of military force; it includes diplomacy, international commerce, and political alliances."

QUESTIONS

1. **What is the relationship between our safety and our happiness?**

   Safety is a prerequisite for happiness. Individuals living in a regime not secure from external threats are unable either to enjoy their rights and liberties fully or to pursue happiness.

2. **What is the Constitution referring to when it speaks of the "common defense"?**

   The common defense consists of funding and regulating

the activities of the armed forces for the sake of protecting the American people from internal and external threats. Congress is responsible for appropriating money to and regulating the military while the president is the commander-in-chief of the armed forces.

5 National Interests, Guided by Justice (pp. 174-176)

There is a fundamental distinction between the United States' national interests and those interests of other nations. Our national interests are those things that benefit our security and prosperity.

The first duty of government is to protect the national interests of the American people. In order to remain an independent nation, the United States cannot allow another nation or international organization to determine its domestic or foreign policy. Although America ought to treat other nations with justice and humanity, national self-interest is a legitimate factor when deliberating particular foreign policy choices.

QUESTIONS

1. **How has America's self-interest influenced its foreign policy choices?**

During the Washington administration, America refrained from participating in Europe's wars in order to strengthen U.S. national defense and economy. During World War II, however, America intervened in the war in Europe because the rise of Nazi Germany threatened the European continent and the United States' security.

2. **What is the relationship between the U.S. national interest and independence?**

Independence requires that neither foreign governments nor international bodies determine the domestic or foreign policy decisions for a nation. The United States government, acting through the proper constitutional institutions and on behalf of the American people, makes the policy decisions affecting the safety and security of the United States.

6 Commerce, Not Conquest (pp. 176-178)

Although a strong military is essential for a nation's security, the Founders sought to engage other nations primarily through international commerce and trade. Commerce with other nations involves the buying and selling of goods. A policy encouraging commerce would favor justice among nations that is evident in honest negotiation and diligent fulfillment of treaties, contracts, and other agreements.

QUESTION

1. **According to the Founders, what were the benefits of international commerce?**

The Founders thought international commerce would both benefit the national economy and encourage peaceful and harmonious relations with other nations. Commerce benefits our economic and security interests, and accords with our system of the rule of law and constitutional government.

7 Justice and Benevolence (pp. 178-181)

Justice and benevolence ought to guide U.S. foreign policy. As a general rule, America should respect other nations' sovereignty by not interfering in their internal political affairs unless its own security is at risk. As in commerce, America should practice justice in its diplomatic engagements, upholding treaties and agreements.

Honesty and good manners in foreign relations is essential to avoiding unnecessary and costly political conflicts. A benevolent foreign policy attempts to maintain peaceful relations with other nations as much as possible. By denouncing a foreign policy of conquest, yet maintaining a strong national defense that discourages foreign antagonism, unnecessary conflict is avoided and prevented. Justice and benevolence also requires the United States to condemn tyranny and uphold liberty in the world.

QUESTION

1. **In addition to serving its own political and economic self-interest, what are the other appropriate features of a prudent and just foreign policy?**

A prudent and just foreign policy ought to respect the sovereignty of other nations, deal fairly and honestly with foreign governments, and advocate the principles of liberty through example and persuasion.

8 The Cause of Liberty in the World

(pp. 181-185)

Promoting liberty throughout the world should be a key component of American foreign policy. Of course, justice and prudence should govern the ways in which America promotes liberty. Establishing an independent government based on the rule of law, natural rights, and the consent of the governed is exceedingly difficult. One nation cannot force liberty onto another. Each nation must choose and accomplish this for itself. Some nations may not have the capacity (at a given time and place) for self-government.

America's duty to promote liberty in the world does not mandate intervention in every case of tyranny or injustice.

INTERVENTIONIST

A person or policy supporting active intervention in the political affairs of other nations.

America must not sacrifice its security in order to free another nation. Prudence must determine particular interventions. At times in American history, a reasoned analysis of the particular circumstances has dictated non-intervention and restraint, such as European wars in the 1790s, or aggressive military engagement in others such as World War I and World War II.

"America's duty to promote liberty in the world does not mandate intervention in every case of tyranny or injustice."

QUESTION

1. **What would the Founders say about the perennial debate between interventionists and non-interventionists?**

The Founders would be reluctant to adopt an idealistic stance either way. They would say that prudence may dictate intervention or non-intervention. Some circumstances will demand neutrality and restraint; others will require more aggressive responses, including military intervention. The prudent foreign policy choice in any given situation is the one that best balances many competing foreign policy considerations: the nation's security and the integrity of its constitutional government, maintaining profitable international trade, upholding treaty obligations, and advancing the cause of liberty, among other core considerations.

SESSION 9

The Command of Our Fortunes: Sovereign Independence and America's Role in the World

Independence Forever (pp. 185-186)

The watchword of American foreign policy is "independence." Independence distinguishes America's interests from those of other nations. Independence maintains the common defense, thereby ensuring the safety of the American people from threats – foreign and domestic. Independence navigates the waters of international diplomacy and trade. Independence, when informed by enduring principles, is a great example of mankind's capacity for self-government under the rule of law.

DIPLOMACY

The various official and unofficial communications, negotiations, and relations between representatives of different nations.

QUESTION

1. What is required for a nation to be truly "independent"?

Independence requires that a nation be free from the rule or control of a power other than itself. An independent nation secures its people from foreign domination. It participates in diplomacy and international trade with other nations in order to benefit its national interests. An independent nation is a self-governing nation committed to the rule of law.

GO DEEPER

Consider the United States' involvement in world affairs today. Would the Founders approve of the degree to which the United States is involved in other nations' affairs? We are often criticized for acting without the support of allies in our foreign policy and for being a bully that acts only in self-interest. How would the Founders have responded to this criticism? What means would the Founders have approved for promoting America's principles around the world?

NOTES:

The
Command of
Our Fortunes:
Sovereign
Independence
and America's
Role in the
World

The Progressive Turn

The year 1987 marked the 200th anniversary of the United States Constitution. The Commission on the Bicentennial invited "every state, city, town and hamlet, every organization and institution, and every family and individual" to celebrate the great occasion with fitting ceremonies, both solemn and festive.

Not everyone agreed. "I cannot accept this invitation," wrote Associate Justice Thurgood Marshall, "for I do not believe that the meaning of the Constitution was forever 'fixed' at the Philadelphia Convention." All of the patriotic celebrations marking the grand event, he wrote, amounted to "little more than a blind pilgrimage to the shrine of the original document now stored in a vault in the National Archives."

In many circles, especially among our intellectual, cultural, and political elites, the principles of America's Founding have been largely abandoned because they are seen as either outdated or defective. The American Founders are more to be departed from than looked up to as a guide for today. America's great founding documents still exist, but they must be disentangled from that past and continually adapted to the future.

How – and why – did this come to be?

What began 100 years ago as an intellectual project made up mostly of academics and independent writers became a popular reform effort under the banner of progressivism. It informed the large-scale political movement of modern liberalism that came to dominate the politics of the 20th century. It continues to shape our politics and confuse the public mind.

If we wish to regain our bearings, we need to understand and come to grips with these changes. If we are to reorient our nation to its first principles, we must understand how deeply these changes have transformed our politics and society – and where, unchecked, they are taking our country.

A NEW REPUBLIC

The Progressive Assault on the Founders' Principles

I N SESSION NINE, we examined the principle of independence that guides America in the world. This completes our study of the principles of the American Founding. Knowing these principles and their meaning is only the first step to understanding America. It is also necessary to comprehend the great challenge to these principles by progressivism and modern liberalism. As you read about this rejection of America's first principles, focus on these key concepts:

Key Concepts

1. In the early 20th century a group of intellectuals known as Progressives rejected the Founding principles.

2. In response to the challenges of industrialization and urbanization, Progressives sought to transform society.

3. Progressivism denies the possibility of self-evident eternal truths.

4. Progressivism also denies the limits on government and sees separation of powers as an obstacle to reform.

5. Because of their rejection of the Declaration, Progressives understand a right as something government grants *to* a

115

citizen, rather than something a citizen has by nature, which government protects.

6. In order to increase their power to remake society, Progressives have tried to undermine private associations in which morality is shaped, and used schools for this end.

7. Progressives have promoted the idea of a "living" Constitution, a doctrine that strips the document of any original meaning and allows it to be interpreted in any way a judge sees fit.

Introduction (pp. 187-188)

Many modern intellectual, cultural, and political elites reject the founding principles as outdated or defective. For these elites, the American Founders offer no guidance for modern life, and the founding documents must be "adapted" to the future. This widespread rejection of America's founding principles stems from the influence of early 20th century progressive intellectuals and authors and their ongoing influence on American political life and political culture.

QUESTION

1. What is the root of the 20th century rejection of American founding principles?

A group of writers and intellectuals known as Progressives launched in the early 20th century a movement that rejected America's founding principles in favor of what they called "progress." This argument forms the basis of modern liberalism.

2 The American Consensus (pp. 188-191)

The challenge of free government is to prevent tyranny while preserving liberty and protecting the rights of the people. The American solution to this challenge was a strong, energetic government; but one founded on core principles of liberty and restrained by a Constitution of limited powers and the rule of law. The consensus created by this arrangement is the bedrock of the American tradition and transcends practical political differences. Although slavery presented a great challenge to the meaning of America's principles, its resolution re-established the meaning of America's principles.

Many in the South promoted slavery – some even called it a "positive good"– as fundamental to the new nation's success. Some claimed that the founding principles did not apply to black people. Others argued that the institution of slavery was incompatible with the principles of the Declaration of Independence. President Abraham Lincoln argued that the Union existed *for* the founding principles. Ultimately, the Union victory in the Civil War preserved and vindicated both these principles and their universal application to all men.

QUESTION

1. **How did Lincoln's political thought and the Civil War amendments represent the completion of the American founding principles?**

Human slavery violated the principles of liberty at the very heart of the American Founding, and abolishing slavery allowed the laws to become fully aligned with those principles. Lincoln argued that the Constitution and the Declaration, once rightly understood, were perfectly compatible and applied to all human beings.

A New Republic (pp. 191-192)

> "The leading figures of the progressive movement argued that the Founders' political order was inadequate to address the changing needs of society."

After the Civil War, the nation prospered. However, the industrial revolution, expansion of America's urban centers, and rise of the United States as a world power instigated a call to rethink and reform virtually all aspects of American life. The theoretical and practical response to these calls was known as progressivism. The leading figures of the progressive movement argued that the Founders' political order was inadequate to address the changing needs of society and the old constitutional order was a failure. (Some saw the Civil War as the inevitable result.) Progressive intellectuals sought new foundational principles and a new political philosophy outside the American political tradition.

QUESTIONS

INDUSTRIAL REVOLUTION

The period of rapid technological change and industrial growth from the late 18th century and into the 19th century that greatly affected many aspects of life in America and around the world.

1. **Why did Progressives seek to transform the principles of American politics?**

   Progressives viewed the founding principles and the American Constitution as inadequate to address the new challenges of the industrial revolution, urban expansion, and America's growing status as a world power.

New (Anti-) Foundational Principles
(pp. 192-196)

> "Progressivism rejected the idea of permanent principles or universal, philosophical ideas."

The new progressive thinking rejected certain fundamental principles of the American Founding. First, progressivism rejected the idea of permanent principles or universal, philosophical ideas. Instead, Progressives argued that truth was always contingent. Progressives believe "self-evident truths" were merely "values" relative to other opinions; they rejected any fixed moral standard, including natural law and natural rights. They favored relativism – the

118

philosophy that all judgments are relative, differing according to events, persons, or circumstances. This view of moral and intellectual relativism renders the arguments of the American Founders meaningless.

Besides rejecting permanent principles, Progressives were historicists – they believed that ideas are relative to historical circumstances. Whatever "values" existed in the past (or the present) are bound to change in the future. Whereas the Founders' understanding of progress relied on certain unchanging standards; Progressives saw progress as change for the sake of change. Holding the view that human nature is not permanent, they relied on modern science to bring about change and progress. They saw themselves as correcting the failures of the American Founding and reorganizing American life to bring about more and more progress. All of this entailed a re-founding of the American political order.

HISTORICISTS
Those who believe that ideas are relative to historical circumstances and evolve in line with historical development.

SESSION 10

A New Republic: The Progressive Assault on the Founders' Principles

QUESTION

1. **How do relativism and historicism lead to a rejection of the American founding principles?**

The American Founding is based on a claim of universal truths that are always and everywhere applicable. Relativism and historicism claim that truth is necessarily variable and historically determined – there are no moral truths that transcend history. The self-evident truths claimed in the American Founding are not true, but merely the products of historical values and changing conditions.

5 A New Theory of Unlimited Government (pp. 196-199)

While the Founders established a limited government that protected natural rights through a written Constitution, Progressives sought to establish a government to bring about "progress." But progress can never be fully realized,

ADMINISTRATIVE STATE

The progressive form of bureaucratic government under which agencies and departments run by "experts" determine and impose most of the rules and regulations imposed by government on society.

DARWINIAN ORGANISM

The idea that government is a living thing in accord with the broader scientific claims of Charles Darwin concerning the evolution and natural selection of all living organisms.

since the future always promises more change. By seeking the limitless goal of progress, Progressives necessarily rejected limited government. Principled limits on government were unnecessary; the extent of government was only a matter of expediency. Rather than asking if government had the power to do something, Progressives asked whether, practically speaking, government *could* do something. The Constitution's mechanisms (federalism, the separation of powers, etc.) were obsolete, obstacles to progress. As a result, there needed to be a new form of unlimited government, called the administrative state, to bring about change and progress.

Rather than a separation of powers, Progressives divided politics (expression of ends) from administration (means to those ends). This transferred the lawmaking power from elected representatives to "objective," "neutral" scientific administrators who were schooled in the progressive ideals and insulated from popular politics. These administrative experts would exercise all powers of government – legislative, executive, and judicial. These agencies alter the law-making process.

Today, Congress delegates its lawmaking power to unaccountable administrative agencies. These agencies issue rules, enforce them, and judge disputes. This administrative state requires a new concept of leadership requiring persuasive communication skills and the ability to direct national progress.

QUESTION

1. **What is the difference between the Founders and Progressives in terms of the end purpose of government?**

For the Founders, the end purpose of government is to protect natural rights. Progressives view government as a Darwinian organism, with no fixed end or purpose, except continually evolving change and unending progress.

6

A New Theory of Rights (pp. 200-203)

In rejecting the founding principles, Progressives developed a new theory of rights. Rights are no longer understood to be natural or permanent claims; they are not derived from "the Laws of Nature and of Nature's God." Progressivism denies human nature as the basis for rights and instead argues that government creates rights to address current problems. According to the Progressives, the Founders' concept of rights did not guarantee social and economic outcomes, but only the right to *pursue* them. In contrast, Progressives wanted to assure equality in the pursuit of happiness, and the progressive welfare state sees its duty as providing happiness by guaranteeing each person's economic security. Such an expansive duty requires vast governmental powers. It also means that government can grant or remove rights as it chooses.

QUESTION

1. How does the progressive understanding of rights differ from the Founders' view?

The Founders understood rights to be independent of government because they pre-existed government – they are natural rights derived from "the Laws of Nature and of Nature's God." Natural rights provide an independent moral standard against which one can judge government, as in the Declaration of Independence. Progressives, in contrast, deny the possibility of natural rights because they deny the existence of a human nature. Government grants rights and removes rights arbitrarily. Rights cannot provide a permanent standard by which to judge government.

"Progressivism denies human nature as the basis for rights and instead argues that government creates rights to address current problems."

SESSION 10

A New Republic: The Progressive Assault on the Founders' Principles

7 A Great National Community

(pp. 204-208)

The progressive theory of government seeks to transform America from a decentralized society with a limited government, free markets, and traditional private associations into a centralized and highly regulated society organized to bring about "social justice" (economic equality). Progressives use the coercive power of government to change sociological conditions and redistribute private wealth. To achieve their ends, Progressives instituted a national income tax and advocated numerous social welfare programs.

The chief obstacle to the progressive transformation of the United States was society itself. The private institutions of civil society promoted local concerns and moral convictions that opposed progressivism. Progressives championed a twofold solution to this problem:

- They advocated "secular knowledge" to diminish the influence of the moral and religious opinions.

- They sought to centralize power away from ordinary citizens and to a centralized national government. Progressives wanted to reduce traditional moral virtues to the status of personal values, to be replaced by a new virtue – faith in government action.

Progressive educational theorists sought to make schools take an active part in directing social change by emancipating Americans from ideas of the past and preparing them for serving the ends of the new state.

> "Progressives use the coercive power of government to change sociological conditions and redistribute private wealth."

Question

1. Why did Progressives seek to "overcome" the institutions of civil society?

The Founders relied on private associations, such as the family and the church, to form the morals and habits necessary for free government. Progressives viewed such moral formation as an obstacle to the changes they sought. Traditional institutions promoted virtues inclined toward self-reliance rather than the collectivism required for national community. Progressive education was to be the key to this social transformation.

8   A New "Living" Constitution (pp. 208-212)

The Founders viewed the court as an institution to uphold the rule of law in the long tradition of American constitutionalism. The court was supposed to be the source of stability, not political change. The court decided cases and controversies that came before them; the legislature and executive branches addressed public policy questions.

Changes in society were to be reflected in the political branches – the legislature and the executive – while the court maintained the supremacy of the Constitution. For Progressives, however, the Constitution was an obstacle to effective administrative government. They sought to transform the Constitution into something more flexible and pliable, which they called a "living" Constitution.

The "living" Constitution doctrine grants the court the power to interpret the document freely – the Constitution means whatever the court says it means. Progressives argued that laws developed according to the needs of the time. Their interpretation transforms judicial power into a form of legislative power. In modern times, the court generally accepts this view.

The Progressives changed the Constitution – not through the constitutional process of amendment, but the interpretative decisions of an appointed court. Originally, judicial review was the process by which the court determined whether positive law conformed to the Constitution. Now, judicial review consists of judges deciding whether the law conforms to their own standards of reason as shaped by developing court decisions.

SESSION 10

A New Republic: The Progressive Assault on the Founders' Principles

"The 'living' Constitution doctrine grants the court the power to interpret the document freely – the Constitution means whatever the court says it means."

QUESTION

1. What is the meaning of a "living" Constitution?

The idea of making the Constitution into a "living" document is to adapt meaning to the time by reinterpreting its text to allow the achievement of ends demanded by changes and progress, regardless of the intent of the Constitution's framers or the consent of the governed.

9 Is It Too Late? (pp. 212-213)

Progressivism presents itself as a prudent response to the challenges of industrialism and urbanization. At its core, however, it rejects both the natural rights teaching of the Declaration and its derivative teachings about limited government. Progressivism has also greatly influenced how we see the world. It provides a new moral imperative: suppressing national interest for the sake of bringing progress to every corner of the earth. As a result, America seems to have moved further and further away from its founding principles. While progressive ideas have by no means eliminated the moral and political teaching of the Founding, the prevalence of progressive arguments – in schools and in the public square – have made it difficult to defend the founding principles.

"Progressivism advocates unlimited government and denies natural rights."

QUESTION

1. How has progressivism challenged the founding principles?

Progressivism advocates unlimited government and denies natural rights. Domestically, it replaces private institutions with public government programs. In foreign policy, it denigrates national interest and uses America's power and influence to bring "progress" to the world.

GO DEEPER

We are often told that today's policies are those the Founders themselves would have favored in today's circumstances. Do you believe this is the case? Why or why not? What changes did Progressives make in our understanding of the Founders' principles? What are the principles that guide the way most policy is made today?

NOTES:

A New
Republic: The
Progressive
Assault on
the Founders'
Principles

A New
Republic: The
Progressive
Assault on
the Founders'
Principles

Another Way Forward

The view of America that dominates the academy, journalism, major foundations, and most segments of the American intellectual community – and as a result, major portions of America's political leadership in both parties – was marked out at the start of the last century by progressive thinkers when they launched their grand project to remake America. We have taken significant steps down this path toward a failed, undemocratic, and illiberal form of statism.

There is another way forward. The slow Europeanization of America is not inevitable, and it's not too late. But it will take a monumental effort to get our country back on track.

We don't need to remake America, or discover new and untested principles. The change we need is not the rejection of America's principles but a great renewal of these permanent truths about man, politics, and liberty – the foundational principles and constitutional wisdom that are the true roots of our country's greatness.

We must look to the principles of the American Founding not as a matter of historical curiosity, but as a source of assurance and direction for our times. In a world of moral confusion, and of arbitrary and unlimited government, the American Founding is our best access to permanent truths and our best ground from which to launch a radical questioning of the whole foundation of the progressive project.

It is not the affirmation of a peculiar set of antiquated claims that tie us to America as much as it is our common recognition of transcendent truths that bind us all together and across time to the patriots of 1776. Only with this sure foundation can we go forward as a nation, addressing the great policy questions before us and continuing to secure the blessings of liberty to ourselves and our posterity.

AMERICAN RENEWAL

The Case for Reclaiming Our Future

NOW THAT WE HAVE REDISCOVERED the philosophical and constitutional American founding principles, and recognized the assault on those principles by progressive liberalism, let's talk about our country's future and how to defend the cause of liberty. While we develop a strategy to reclaim America's future, consider the following key concepts:

Key Concepts

1. Progressivism is largely responsible for American's crisis of confidence by having publicly attacked the legitimacy of the founding principles and reduced the Constitution to a "living," and largely meaningless, document.

2. The progressive welfare state promotes habits of dependency; a return to limited government would revive virtues required for self-government.

3. American renewal depends on recalling our first principles and revitalizing our civic knowledge. We must also reign in financially irresponsible government, unravel the administrative state and return to federalism, and hold government officials accountable to the terms in the Constitution.

4. American economic prosperity relies on free markets.

5. Patriotic Americans can revive our core principles and safeguard American constitutionalism for future generations.

> "American renewal depends on recalling our first principles and revitalizing our civic knowledge."

1 Introduction (pp. 215-216)

The greatest threats to American liberty are not external, but internal. The American people are hard-working, wealthy, religious, and generous. The American economy comprises almost 25 percent of world gross domestic product. The military extends the United States' power around the world. Yet, as a nation, the United States seems bent on self-destruction.

> "Our once-limited government now presses itself into nearly every sphere of private life."

Our once-limited government now presses itself into nearly every sphere of private life, restricted only by expediency rather than principle. Congress today passes legislation with little deliberation, and creates bureaucracies that exercise legislative, executive, and judicial power. The courts no longer judge disputes under the law — they override the constitutional authority of the political branches and rewrite the law. The new administrative power of Congress and the new legislative power of the Supreme Court prevents the modern executive from controlling the execution of the law. Citizens have become consumers paying higher taxes for more government services. Government continues to spend money irresponsibly, leaving the bill for future generations.

QUESTION

1. **How have Progressives transformed the legislature, executive, and judiciary?**

The legislature no longer actually legislates. Congress grants power to administrative agencies to regulate specific policy areas. Not only do these administrative agencies exercise legislative power but also executive and judicial power. The judicial branch has adopted the "living" Constitution doctrine, which allows judges to legislate from the bench. Meanwhile, the executive attempts to rule over a vast federal bureaucracy that is largely independent from both the executive and Congress.

2 A New Form of Despotism? (pp. 217-219)

The modern welfare state promotes dependency, undermining the independence and self-reliance that are the hallmarks of free government. Citizens become clients of government, and government programs are payoffs to voter groups. As this culture of dependency expands to encompass basic human needs, as well as the material goods of a middle class lifestyle, a conflict emerges between the demands of shortsighted self-interest and the long-term common good.

In this era, there is new despotism on the rise that is the product of a democratic love of equality and centralized regulation of government. By fostering dependency through welfare programs and promoting petty and selfish interests, government destroys the moral character required for self-government. People exchange liberty and self-reliance for the comfortable security of perpetual childhood. This creates a new, soft despotism – a despotism suited for people who love equality of outcome more than freedom.

QUESTION

1. What is soft despotism? How does it parallel with progressive reforms?

Soft despotism occurs when citizens exchange the independent character of a self-governing people for the child-like, comfortable security provided by government. In using government to control and remake society, progressive reformers encourage dependency on the state as a replacement for the private institutions that foster independent and self-reliant moral character. Although it is less harsh, government that does more and more to control our lives is still despotic.

"By fostering dependency through welfare programs and promoting petty and selfish interests, government destroys the moral character required for self-government."

CONCLUSION

American Renewal: The Case for Reclaiming Our Future

3 The Path of Decline (pp. 219-220)

American politics has always involved debate, not just about partisan issues, but about how we understand ourselves. The view of America presented today in the media, schools, and most of the intellectual community, however, is antithetical to the American founding principles. As a society, we have moved far down the progressive path. To see the end-result of this path, we need only look to modern Europe. These increasingly socialized nations have suffered serious decline. Europeans have lost confidence in their own civilization and are mostly unwilling to defend themselves intellectually or militarily. In contrast to the progressive and European view, the Founders understood there is no true progress beyond the enduring truths enshrined in the Declaration of Independence and the Constitution.

> "Europeans have lost confidence in their own civilization and are mostly unwilling to defend themselves intellectually or militarily."

QUESTION

1. **What are some of the destructive consequences of the progressive path that can be seen in Europe today?**

In Europe, birth rates are declining, people lack the self-reliant and independent spirit that the American Founders prized, administrative agencies regulate every aspect of life, and international institutions have supplanted national sovereignty.

4 The Promise of American Renewal

(pp. 221-222)

Europe's present is not necessarily America's future. Though the parallels are clear, the United States still maintains a political culture grounded in American constitutionalism. America's founding principles are still a source of moral and political guidance. Renewing these principles is the way to get America back on track. In a world of moral confusion, and of arbitrary and unlimited government, these principles are our best access to permanent truths. The founding principles are our best ground from which to launch a radical questioning of the whole foundation of the progressive project to remake America.

"America's founding principles are still a source of moral and political guidance."

QUESTION

1. **Why has the progressive project not been wholly successful in the United States?**

Despite Progressives' attacks on the founding principles, the American people are still largely a religious, hard-working, and self-reliant people who shun dependency in favor of liberty and republican self-government. While Progressives have attacked these virtues, they have not destroyed them. Most Americans may be confused today about the modern meaning and application of founding principles. But they still retain a commitment to America's principles and institutions.

CONCLUSION

American Renewal: The Case for Reclaiming Our Future

5 Educating for Liberty (pp. 222-224)

There is a crisis in U.S. citizenship. Schools largely delegitimize the American founding principles; students complete degrees at elite colleges without ever taking a course in American history. Historicism and relativism rule the academy. As a result, the founding principles are often ignored or distorted.

The solution to this crisis rests in teaching America's first principles at all levels of our educational system. Civic education needs to make the principled argument for democratic republicanism, and this requires teachers trained in American history, government, and constitutionalism.

"The solution to this crisis rests in teaching America's first principles at all levels of our educational system."

Reforming legal education is also important. For decades, law schools have advocated the progressive "living" Constitution, rather than upholding the traditional view of the courts and the Constitution itself. We must reverse course and commit ourselves at every level of education to promote awareness and appreciation of founding principles.

QUESTION

1. **What educational crisis does America face? What is the solution?**

Many citizens do not know the principles on which our government is established. The American people are inwardly attracted to the founding principles. The problem today is that students and citizens are not being taught these principles.

6 An Expression of the American Mind (pp. 224-226)

Civic education should not end in the classroom. Participatory government requires public deliberation. Public discussion, even among our leaders, has moved from serious consideration of political principles to narrow, partisan quibbling over political leaders' short-term gains.

Despite constant criticism by academic elites, politicians, and the media, most Americans still believe in the uniqueness of this country and respect its noble ideas. We need to defend our principles. We must apply these principles creatively to modern problems, supporting positions consistent with them.

We must reject the progressive understanding of rights as government-granted entitlements. Rights are inherent to man's nature; they are not products of government.

> "Despite constant criticism by academic elites, politicians, and the media, most Americans still believe in the uniqueness of this country and respect its noble ideas."

We must retrieve and renew the principles enshrined in the Declaration of Independence and replace the "living" Constitution argument with the Founders' Constitution of limited government.

QUESTION

1. **Part of the American political crisis stems from a crisis in public civic education. What is the solution to this problem?**

Private associations of students, alumni, and faculty must call for a return to the earlier method of education. Scholars ought to make public arguments in favor of America's founding principles.

7 A New Era of Constitutional Responsibility (pp. 226-228)

We need political leaders who understand and uphold America's principles. Public officials take a solemn oath to support the Constitution, which means they have a moral obligation to abide by the founding document in carrying out the duties of office. For members of Congress, this means determining constitutional authority for bills they pass. For the president, it means considering the constitutionality of legislation, withholding approval of bills deemed unconstitutional, and executing the law in a constitutional manner. Judges are in a unique position to spell out the meaning and consequences of the Constitution. However, it is imperative to understand – and for judges to recognize – they are not above, outside, or immune from the constraints of that document.

Much of government's work occurs *outside* the three branches in unaccountable administrative agencies and government bureaucracies. Congress must reclaim their legislative authority from them. Congress should

> "We need political leaders who understand and uphold America's principles."

re-evaluate the necessity, purpose, and effectiveness of these agencies on a regular basis. Members of all three branches should justify all that they do in terms of the Constitution.

QUESTIONS

1. Why is it inappropriate for the Supreme Court to rely on foreign law?

To rely on foreign law is a violation of the consent principle to be governed by anything outside of America's system of constitutional government.

2. How does the congressional grant of power to administrative agencies represent a challenge to American constitutionalism?

Congress gives lawmaking power to unelected and largely unaccountable bureaucrats. These bureaucrats exercise executive and judicial authority in specific policy areas. Insulated from both the President and the Congress, the administrative state operates without consent of the American people.

8

Defending Free Markets and Fiscal Responsibility (pp. 229-231)

The right to pursue and possess private property is a source of opportunity, a measure of liberty, and a practical means to pursue happiness. For the Founders, government established the rule of law and provided the framework in which opportunity and prosperity could thrive. Government provided incentives to work hard in order to keep the fruits of one's labor. Civil society benefited from the free market that allowed people to pursue their own self-interests as well as the common interest.

The right to property is under assault, and needs protection. Excessive government involvement in the free

> "The right to pursue and possess private property is a source of opportunity, a measure of liberty, and a practical means to pursue happiness."

market is counterproductive. Taxes and regulations burden commerce. Politicians continue to spend taxpayer money irresponsibly. Economic recovery programs that grant government control over large portions of the economy produce more long-term harm than good. If America is to be financially secure, entitlement reform and fiscal discipline are the first steps.

QUESTION

1. Why must fiscal irresponsibility be reined in?

Government spending has tripled in the last 20 years. By 2052, all tax money will be devoted to funding 100 percent of already existing social welfare programs. This moment may arrive sooner if more entitlement programs are added.

9 The Revival of Self-Government

(pp. 231-235)

In assuming more tasks in more areas outside its responsibilities, modern government has greatly damaged American self-rule. By promoting an entitlement mentality and dependency rather than self-reliance and independence, administrative government encourages a character that is incompatible with republicanism. The state's extended reach continues to push traditional social institutions into the shadows. We must reverse this trend and restore the standing and influence of social institutions meant to strengthen culture and civil society.

We must defend the family, as the nursery of citizenship and virtue. Restoring the role of religion in American life requires changing current assumptions about the radical separation of church and state. To return to federalism, states, communities, neighborhoods, families, and individuals must reclaim their authority from bureaucrats.

"In assuming more tasks in more areas outside its responsibilities, modern government has greatly damaged American self-rule."

137

Education is especially ripe for reform. Decentralizing education would encourage innovation and competition and promote local involvement, which promotes self-reliance, a sense of community and common good, and the virtues appropriate for free government. Patriotism, and an enlightened love of liberty, is also essential for free government's survival.

QUESTION

1. **The Progressive view of governing has transformed most spheres of American political and civic life. What obstacles must we overcome to restore self-government?**

The progressive program of entitlement and social welfare programs has fostered dependency. Historicism and relativism has led to a public amorality that equates the pursuit of pleasure with freedom. To revive self-government and its moral pre-conditions, we must dismantle progressive institutions, including its centralized administrative bureaucracy.

10 Upholding Liberty in the World

(pp. 235-237)

By the very nature of the principles upon which the Founders established it, the United States – more than any other nation in history – has a responsibility to defend not only the cause of liberty but the meaning of liberty at home and abroad.

A major purpose of American constitutionalism is to provide for the common defense. The United States must be willing and able at all times to defend itself against conventional and unconventional threats. Weapons of mass destruction in the hands of rogue nations and terrorists compel the U.S. government to actively defend our country. The United States must secure its borders, preserve its tradition of constitutionalism, and promote the long-term prosperity of its people. This requires a defense of the ideas and principles that all Americans hold in common – the universal principles of the Declaration of Independence – as well as a commitment to our national sovereignty and independence.

America must reclaim a sense of identity. In order to become an American citizen, immigrants should demonstrate an understanding of the principles of free government. Immigrants hopeful of becoming citizens should be able to speak our common language and possess good moral character.

American policy must make the case for American principles of economic and political liberty, as well as the constitutional institutions to secure that liberty. It must also challenge the denial of these principles by threats, such as transnational populism or radical Islam.

QUESTION

1. **What is public diplomacy? Why does America need to engage in it in today's dangerous world of international affairs?**

Public diplomacy is a public argument in defense of America's principles and institutions, especially to those throughout the world who deny these universal principles.

CONCLUSION

American Renewal: The Case for Reclaiming Our Future

"The American Founders understood that liberty is hard to attain and even more difficult to keep."

11 Our Noble Task (pp. 238-239)

The American Founders understood that liberty is hard to attain and even more difficult to keep. Still, they boldly placed their lives, fortunes, and sacred honor on the line. We can reclaim the liberty that Americans since the Revolution have fought and died to preserve. Our principles can be rediscovered, and our Constitution can be preserved. This is the task Americans face in the 21st century: to reclaim and preserve the liberty that is our birthright.

GO DEEPER

What are some of the first steps to reclaiming American liberty that you can take? How would you start teaching others about the principles of the American Founding?

NOTES:

CONCLUSION

American
Renewal:
The Case for
Reclaiming Our
Future